Upper-Intermediate

WORLD PASS

Expanding English Fluency

Susan Stempleski
James R. Morgan
Nancy Douglas
Kristin L. Johannsen

HEINLE
CENGAGE Learning™

Australia • Brazil • Japan • Korea • Mexico • Singapore • Spain • United Kingdom • United States

World Pass Upper-Intermediate,
Combo Split A
Susan Stempleski
James R. Morgan, Nancy Douglas,
Kristin L. Johannsen

Publisher: Christopher Wenger
Director of Content Development:
Anita Raducanu
Director of Product Marketing: Amy Mabley
Acquisitions Editor: Mary Sutton-Paul
Developmental Editor: Rebecca Klevberg
Associate Editor: Christine Galvin-Combet
Editiotial Assistant: Bridget McLaughlin
Content Project Manager: Tan Jin Hock
Sr. Print Buyer: Mary Beth Hennebury
International Marketing Manager: Ian Martin
Contributing Development Editor:
Ellen Kisslinger
Compositor: CHROME Media Pte. Ltd.
Photo Researcher: Christopher Hanzie
Illustrator: Raketshop Design Studio
(Philippines)
Cover/Text Designer: CHROME Media Pte. Ltd.
Cover Images: Corbis

Text Credits
Page 7: "Rules of the Game," from THE JOY LUCK CLUB by Amy
Tan, copyright ©1989 by Amy Tan. Used by permission of G.P.
Putnam's Sons, a division of Penguin Group (USA) Inc.; page 8:
Adapted from "The Monkey's Paw" (1902) from *The Lady of the
Barge 6th ed.* Published in 1906 by W.W. Jacobs, Harper & Brothers,
Publishers, London and New York; page 76: Adapted from "Gorilla-
Suited Prankster Caught," Ananova.com, October 13, 2004. Used by
permission of Ananova, Ltd.

Photo Credits
Unless otherwise stated, all photos are from PhotoDisc, Inc. Digital
Imagery © copyright 2005 PhotoDisc, Inc. and CHROME Media Pte.
Ltd. Photos from other sources:
page 4: (top) Royalty-Free/CORBIS, (bottom) Richard T. Nowitz/
CORBIS; page 5: Janet Jarman/CORBIS; page 6: Gabe Palmer/CORBIS;
page 21: METRO AG; page 29: Royalty-Free/CORBIS; page 30:
(bottom) Royalty-Free/CORBIS; page 43: Arko Datta/Reuters/Landov;
page 53: Royalty-Free/CORBIS; page 54: (left) Jim Thompson House &
Museum, (right) Chris Lisle/CORBIS; page 55: Jim Thompson House &
Museum; page 56: Randy Faris/CORBIS

The CNN® logo is a registered trademark of CNN:
© & ® 2005. Cable News Network LP, LLLP. A Time
Warner Company. All Rights Reserved.

Every effort has been made to trace all sources of
illustrations/photos/information in this book, but
if any have been inadvertently overlooked, the
publisher will be pleased to make the necessary
arrangements at the first opportunity.

For permission to use material from this text or product,
submit all requests online at **www.cengage.com/permissions**
Further permissions questions can be emailed to
permissionrequest@cengage.com

ISBN-13: 978-1-4130-1088-6

ISBN-10: 1-4130-1088-1

Heinle
25 Thomson Place
Boston, Massachusetts 02210
USA

Cengage Learning is a leading provider of customized learning solutions with
office locations around the globe, including Singapore, the United Kingdom,
Australia, Mexico, Brazil and Japan. Locate our local office at:
international.cengage.com/region

Cengage Learning products are represented in Canada by Nelson Education, Ltd.

Visit Heinle online at **elt.heinle.com**
Visit our corporate website at **cengage.com**

Printed in China by China Translation & Printing Services Limited
4 5 6 7 8 9 10 09

Acknowledgments

We would firstly like to thank the educators who provided invaluable feedback throughout the development of the *World Pass* series:

Carmen Pulido Alcaraz, Instituto Cultural Mexico-Norteamericano, Guadalajara; Maria Isabel de Souza Lima Baracat, Centro de Comunicação Inglesa, Garça; João Alfredo Bergmann, Instituto Cultural Brasileiro Norte-Americano, Porto Alegre; Elisabeth Blom, Casa Thomas Jefferson, Brasília; Flávia Carneiro - Associação Brasil América; Salvador Enriquez Casteñeda, Instituto Cultural Mexico-Norteamericano, Guadalajara; Ronaldo Couto, SBS, São Paulo; Maria Amélia Carvalho Fonseca, Centro Cultural Brasil-Estados Unidos, Belém; Henry W. Grant, Centro Cultural Brasil-Estados Unidos, Campinas; Leticia Adelina Ruiz Guerrero, ITESO, Guadalajara; Brian Lawrence Kilkenny, PrepaTec, Guadalajara; Lunalva de Fátima Lacerda, Cooplem, Brasília; Raquel Lambert, CCBEU - Centro Cultural Brasil Estados Unidos de Franca; Alberto Hernandez Medina, M. Ed., Tecnológico de Monterrey, Guadalajara; Michelle Merritt-Ascencio, University of Guadalajara; Evania A. Netto, ICBEU - São José dos Campos; Janette Carvalhinho de Oliveira, Universidade Federal do Espírito Santo, Vitória; Ane Cibele Palma, CCBEU/Interamericano, Curitiba; Danielle Rêgo, ICBEU - MA; Marie Adele Ryan, Associação Alumni, São Paulo; Hector Sanchez, PROULEX, Guadalajara; Dixie Santana, Universidad Panamericana, Guadalajara; Rodrigo Santana, CCBEU/Goiânia; Debora Schisler, SEVEN English & Español, São Paulo; Sávio Siqueira, ACBEU Salvador; Eric Tejeda, PROULEX, Guadalajara; Carlos Eduardo Tristão, DISAL; Joaquin Romero Vázquez, Tec de Monterrey, Guadalajara; Liliana Villalobos ME, Universidad Marista de Guadalajara, Universidad de Guadalajara

---

A great many people participated in the making of the *World Pass* series. In particular I would like to thank the authors, Nancy Douglas and James Morgan, for all their hard work, creativity, and good humor. I also extend special thanks to development editor Ellen Kisslinger. Thanks are also due to publisher Chris Wenger, acquisitions editor Mary Sutton-Paul, and all the other wonderful people at Heinle who have worked so hard on this project. I am also very grateful to the many reviewers around the world, whose insightful comments on early drafts of the *World Pass* materials were much appreciated.

Susan Stempleski

We'd like to extend a very special thank you to Chris Wenger at Heinle for spearheading the project and providing leadership, support, and guidance throughout the development of the series. Jean Pender and Ellen Kisslinger edited our materials with speed, precision, and a sense of humor. Susan Stempleski's extensive experience was reflected in her invaluable feedback that helped to shape the material in this book.

Thanks also go to those on the editorial, production, and support teams who helped to make this book happen: Anita Raducanu, Sally Giangrande, Jin-Hock Tan, Bridget McLaughlin, Christine Galvin-Combet, Rebecca Klevberg, Mary Sutton-Paul, and their colleagues in Asia and Latin America.

I would also like to thank my parents Alexander and Patricia, for their love and encouragement and to my husband Jorge and daughter Jasmine—thank you for your patience and faith in me. I couldn't have done this without you!
Nancy Douglas

I would also like to thank my mother, France P. Morgan, for her unflagging support and my father, Lee Morgan Jr., for instilling the love of language and learning in me.
James R. Morgan

I would like to thank my husband, Kevin Millham, for his support and saintly patience.
Kristin L. Johannsen

To the Student

Welcome to *World Pass*! The main goal of this two-level, upper-intermediate/advanced level series is to help you increase your fluency in English. By fluency, I mean the ability to say what you want in more than one way, and to communicate your ideas clearly, confidently, and easily. To help students increase their fluency, *World Pass* focuses on dynamic vocabulary building, essential grammar, and stimulating listening, speaking, and writing activities that emphasize the language people need for real world communication. Features of *World Pass* that emphasize the development of oral and written fluency include the following:

- Vocabulary Focus sections. A *Vocabulary Focus* section opens each of the 12 main units and presents topic-related vocabulary along with opportunities to practice using the new words and expressions in a variety of ways. The section includes a "Vocabulary Builder" activity that helps you expand your vocabulary through the use of a particular vocabulary-building tool (e.g., words families, root words, or compound nouns). Many of the *Vocabulary Focus* sections conclude with an "Ask & Answer" task that can be used as a basis for discussion by pairs, groups, or whole classes of students, and provides opportunities to actively use new vocabulary to express personal ideas, opinions, and experiences.

- Listening sections. To become a fluent speaker, you need to be a fluent listener. These sections provide opportunities for you to improve your listening comprehension through active practice with a variety of materials, such as interviews, news reports, and discussions. For added conversational fluency practice, each *Listening* section ends with an "Ask & Answer" discussion task.

- Language Focus sections. These sections focus on essential grammar points and provide opportunity for fluency practice through a wide variety of activity types, from more controlled exercises to more personalized, free-response type activities and open-ended communication tasks such as role plays or interviews.

- Speaking sections. Each of these sections presents a specific speaking skill or strategy and outlines a communicative activity that help you to develop your fluency by providing opportunities for you to use new language and vocabulary items in a natural way.

- Writing sections. Each of these sections in *World Pass* provide instruction and practice with different kinds of writing such as, business and personal letters, summarizing information, and persuasive writing.

- Communication sections. The *Communication* sections that conclude each main unit consolidate and review the language material presented in the unit. Communication tasks vary widely and contribute to the development of fluency by focusing on meaningful speaking practice in activities such as games, presentations, interviews, and discussions.

- Expansion Pages. Each unit of *World Pass* is followed by *Expansion Pages*. The *Expansion Pages* are designed for students who want to learn additional vocabulary on their own and to have additional practice with the words and expressions presented in the units. Because the *Expansion Pages* are meant for self-study, they consist of exercises that you can do independently and then check your own answers.

SOME LANGUAGE LEARNING TIPS

Becoming a fluent speaker of English can be challenging, but it can also be a highly rewarding experience. Here are a few tips to help you make the most of the experience.

To increase your vocabulary:
- **Keep a vocabulary log.** Keep a list of new vocabulary items in the back pages of a notebook. From time to time, count up the number of words you have learned. You will be surprised at how quickly the number increases.
- **Use new words in sentences.** To fix news words in your mind, put them into sentences of your own. Do the maximum, not the minimum, with new vocabulary.
- **Make flashcards.** Create vocabulary flashcards that allow you to categorize, label, personalize, and apply new words. Put the words and their definitions on individual cards. Include a sample sentence that shows how the word is used in context.

To improve your speaking skills:

- **Read aloud.** Reading examples and texts out loud is a way of gaining confidence in speaking and letting the patterns of English "sound in your head." Even speaking out loud to yourself can be good practice.
- **Record yourself speaking.** Try recording yourself whenever you can. When you listen to the recording afterwards, don't worry if you sound hesitant or have made mistakes. If you do this several times, you will find that each version is better than the last.

To improve your reading skills:

- **Read passages more than once.** Reading the same reading passage several times will help you increase your reading speed and improve your fluency.
- **Summarize what you read.** When you summarize, you tell the main facts or ideas without giving all the details. Summarizing is a good way to be sure you really understand what you have read.

To improve your writing skills:

- **Increase the amount of writing you do.** For example, you might keep a personal diary in English, write small memos to yourself, or write a summary of a reading passage. The more you write, the more fluent and error-free your writing will become.
- **Analyze different types of writing.** Look at examples of different types of writing you may want to do: essays, formal letters, e-mail messages. Notice the form of the writing and think about what you could imitate to increase your fluency in writing.

To improve your listening comprehension:

- **Listen to recorded material several times.** You aren't expected to understand everything the first time your hear it. If you listen several times, you will probably understand something new each time.
- **Predict what you will hear.** Try to guess what you will hear before you listen. This will help you to focus while you listen and understand more of what you hear.

As you complete each unit of *World Pass*, ask yourself the questions on the **Learning Tips Checklist** below to keep track of the tips you are using and to remind yourself to try using others. To become a truly fluent speaker of English, you will need to practice the different language skills in a variety of ways. Find out what ways work best for you and use them to your advantage.

Susan Stempleski

Sincerely,
Susan Stempleski

Learning Tips Checklist
Which language learning tips did you use as you worked through the unit? Note the ones you used and think about which were most helpful. As you work through the next unit, continue using the helpful ones and try using ones you haven't yet implemented.

Did you . . .

- ❏ record new words in a vocabulary log?
- ❏ try using new words in sentences?
- ❏ make and use vocabulary flashcards?
- ❏ read aloud as often as you could?
- ❏ record and listen to yourself speaking?
- ❏ read reading passages more than once?
- ❏ summarize what you read?
- ❏ write a lot and frequently?
- ❏ analyze and imitate different types of writing?
- ❏ listen to recorded material several times?
- ❏ predict what you would hear before you listened?

What's the Story?

Lesson A | The story of my life

1 VOCABULARY FOCUS

What's the story?

People use the word *story* in many different ways, for example, a *news story* or a *bedtime story*. What are some other ways people use *story*? Make a list and tell the class.

A Read these four short conversations. Who do you think might have these conversations? Where might the people be?

1. A: What's his <u>story</u>?
   B: He says he was at home watching TV when the robbery occurred.

2. A: I don't want to hear any more <u>stories</u> out of you, young man!
   B: But it's true! I didn't eat all the cookies. I swear!

3. A: What's the magazine's cover <u>story</u> this week?
   B: The Olympics. The Games are big news right now.

4. A: How was the movie?
   B: The special effects were excellent, but the <u>story</u> was too predictable.

B Pair work. **Look at the conversations in A. How is the word *story* used in each one? Match each use with its definition.**

<u>3</u> an article or report in a newspaper or magazine
<u>4</u> the events in a book, movie, or person's life
<u>1</u> an alibi
<u>2</u> a fabricated description of events

C Pair work. **Read what the three people in the pictures are saying. Pay attention to the words in blue.**

We had two suspects. I believed the first guy. We could verify his story easily—all the facts made sense. The second guy was completely inconsistent and was always altering his story. All the facts were conflicting. You can usually tell when someone is making up a story. It just doesn't seem real.

I could go after a lot of stories. There are many choices, but I have to pick one. Personally, I like to cover the stories about politics. Of course, before a story is published, I have to go over it and make sure the facts are accurate. That part of the job is boring.

People interpret my short stories in different ways. Everyone has their own opinion about what they mean. My stories are complex. You have to piece together the story and figure out who you think the criminal is.

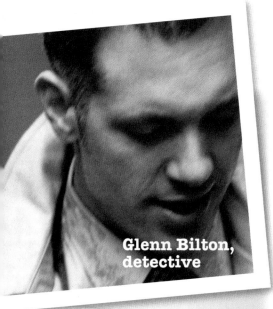

Glenn Bilton, detective

Cassandra Chu, news reporter

Patricia Adams, mystery author

D Place the verbs in blue in C into the chart below.

Meaning	Verb
1. inventing something (to fool someone)	making up
2. review	
3. figure out what happened	
4. analyze (to get the meaning)	
5. changing	
6. report a news story	
7. pursue an idea	
8. check to see if something is true	

▶ **Ask & *Answer***

Have you ever made up a story? Have you ever told a white lie (an untrue story told to avoid hurting someone's feelings)?

▶▶ **Vocabulary Builder** ▲▲

All the verbs in C are used with the word *story*. Other verbs, such as *kill* and *change*, are also used with *story*. What do you think those phrases mean? What other verbs can be used with *story*?

2 LISTENING

Everybody has a story.

A Pair work. Al Benning, a professor in the anthropology department at UCLA, is doing a community research project called "Everybody Has a Story." What do you think it's about? Tell your partner.

EVERYBODY HAS A STORY.

B Pair work. Listen. Take notes and then answer these questions with a partner. (CD Track 01)

1. What is the "Everybody Has a Story" booth and how does it work?

   _____

   _____

2. What is the story booth's purpose?

   _____

   _____

C Listen again to Mary's story only. Complete the chart. (CD Track 02)

1. Year she started working in café	
2. What she did in the café in the 50s	
3. What she wasn't allowed to do	
4. What she does in the café now	

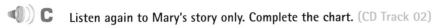

▶ **Ask & Answer**

Why is Mary's personal story important?
What historical information does it give us?

3 LANGUAGE FOCUS

Review of the simple past and present perfect

A Clive Edwards is a journalist. Read about his life and notice the highlighted verb forms. Then read the sentences below and circle the correct answers.

> My father worked as a journalist for over thirty years. He died ten years ago. I've also worked as a journalist for my entire career. It's a wonderful job. I worked for CNN in the 1990s, and now I work for The Sun Times. I've reported from countries in Asia, Africa, and South America. I've seen a lot of exciting situations. I just received my new assignment. They want to send me to Mexico City. I don't know if I'll accept it. I haven't decided yet.

1. The sentence "My father <u>worked</u> as a journalist . . ." tells us that Clive's father is still / no longer a journalist.
2. The sentence "I've also <u>worked</u> as a journalist . . ." tells us that Clive is still / no longer a journalist.
3. The sentence "I <u>worked</u> for CNN . . ." tells us about a specific point / non-specific time in Clive's work history.
4. The sentence "I've <u>reported</u> from countries . . ." tells us about a specific point / non-specific time in Clive's work history.
5. The sentence "I've <u>seen</u> a lot of exciting situations" tells us that Clive is talking about a repeated action / something that happened once in the indefinite past.
6. The sentence "I <u>haven't decided yet</u>," shows that the present perfect + *not yet* is used to talk about things that have not happened before now / happened at a specific time in the past.

B Read this radio interview with journalist Clive Edwards.
Write the simple past or present perfect form of the verb in parentheses.

Interviewer: Today's guest is Mr. Clive Edwards. He
_____ (1. graduate) summa cum laude
from Brown University in 1991. Today he is an
award-winning journalist for the XPTV Network. How
long _____ you _____ (2. work) as a
reporter?

Clive: More than fifteen years.

Int: Mr. Edwards, what _____ (3. be) your most
memorable experience to date?

CE: I _____ (4. go after) many stories in my career,
but the one about the international space station
_____ (5. be) the most memorable. In fact, I'm
still covering that story as it continues to develop.

Int: You _____ (6. visit) some dangerous places in
the 1990s.

CE: Yes, I did. I often _____ (7. go) to war zones.

Int: _____ you _____ (8. choose) where you
would be assigned?

CE: No. I just _____ (9. go) wherever I was told.

Int: _____ you ever _____ (10. feel)
scared on the job?

CE: Of course. Just last year a bomb _____
(11. explode) near me. That _____ (12. is)
terrifying.

Int: _____ you ever _____ (13. be)
injured?

CE: Fortunately, no. I'm happy to say I _____ never
_____ (14. be) hurt at all! It's amazing
considering some of the things I've done to get a story!

Int: Yesterday you _____ (15. win) the "Courage in
Journalism" award. Congratulations!

CE: Thanks.

C Pair work. Act out the role play.

Student A: Imagine you are a famous person from
one of the following fields or one of your own.
Tell your partner your name.

entertainment	sports
politics	other: _____

Student B: You are a journalist interviewing a famous
person. Think of three or four questions to ask your
famous partner and conduct an interview.

How long have you . . . ?
When did you first . . . ?
What has been your most memorable . . . ?
Have you ever . . . ?

D Pair work. Switch roles and do the role play again.

4 SPEAKING

Did I ever tell you about the time . . . ?

A Put the events of the story in order. Notice the expressions in **blue** that are used when telling a story.

a. <u>2</u> **It happened when** we were living in an old house on Beach Street. Everyone in the neighborhood said it was haunted, but we just laughed and ignored them.

b. <u>4</u> I was shocked at what I saw! The living room furniture was in different positions! My wife immediately said, "A ghost moved our furniture!" Then we heard a noise from the closet. **In the end**, it wasn't a ghost after all. We opened the door and saw my cousin hiding there. He was playing a joke on us.

c. <u>1</u> **Did I ever tell you about the time** there was a ghost in our house?

d. <u>5</u> **It seems funny now, but** at the time we were really scared!

e. <u>3</u> **One night** however, we were asleep in our bedrooms upstairs. **Suddenly**, we heard some loud thumping noises downstairs. At first, I was too sleepy to do anything about it. But finally, I went downstairs to investigate.

World Link

An ogre fights a dragon with the help of a talking donkey and then marries a beautiful princess? Old news! The storyline from the hit movie *Shrek* is exciting, but nothing new. A hero facing a challenge, meeting a magical helper, and being rewarded are all examples of "universal themes"—story concepts that can be found almost anywhere in the world!

B Write each expression from **A** under an appropriate category in the chart below.

Introducing the story	Giving general background information	
I'll never forget the time . . .	A couple of years ago . . . *One night*	
<u>Did I ever tell you about the time . . .</u>	Last summer . . . *we heard*	

Introducing the action	Ending the story	Reflecting back on the story
All of a sudden . . .	What happened in the end was . . . *It wasn't a ghost*	Looking back on it, . . . *It seems funny now but*

C Pair work. Think of a time when one of these things happened. Then tell your partner a story about it. Use the expressions from **B**.

- You saw something scary.
- You lost something important.
- You did something very embarrassing/funny/risky.
- Your idea: _____

> I'll never forget the time I lost my house keys. It was a couple of years ago . . .

Listening to a story

Showing you're listening:
Wow!   *Are you kidding?*
Really!   *Are you joking?*
Unbelievable!

Asking follow-up questions:
And then what happened?
What did you do next?

Interrupting to clarify:
Do you mean?
Did you say?

What's the Story?

Lesson B | Tell me a story.

1 GET READY TO READ

The moral of the story

Do you have a favorite story? What is it?
What is it about? Does it teach a lesson?

A Pair work. **Read this excerpt from Amy Tan's book** *The Joy Luck Club***. Then answer the questions below with a partner.**

1. What's the moral of this story?
2. Do you agree with this lesson? Why or why not?
3. Have you ever done something that you were warned not to do? What happened?

"Do not ride your bicycle around the corner," the mother had told her daughter when she was seven.

"Why not!" protested the girl.

"Because then I cannot see you and you will fall down and cry and I will not hear you."

"How do you know I'll fall?" whined the girl.

"It is in a book, *The Twenty-Six Malignant Gates*, all the bad things that can happen to you outside the protection of this house."

"I don't believe you. Let me see the book."

"It is written in Chinese. You cannot understand it. That is why you must listen to me."

"What are they, then?" the girl demanded. Tell me the twenty-six bad things."

But the mother sat knitting in silence.

"What twenty-six!" shouted the girl.

The mother still did not answer her.

"You can't tell me because you don't know! You don't know anything!" And the girl ran outside, jumped on her bicycle, and in her hurry to get away, she fell before she even reached the corner.

B Pair work. **The words and phrases below are all in the reading on page 9. What do you think the story excerpt is going to be about? Tell your partner. Then read the story excerpt and see if your ideas were correct.**

> stormy night   family   visitor   magic charm   wish   fate

2 READING

The Monkey's Paw

A Read the excerpt from the story "The Monkey's Paw" on page 9.
Then number the events from the story in the correct order.

4 Mr. White uses the monkey's paw to make a wish.
7 Mr. and Mrs. White receive some money.
1 Sergeant-Major Morris returns from traveling overseas.
5 Herbert goes to work.
2 Morris visits the White family and shows them a monkey's paw.
3 Morris tries to destroy the monkey's paw.
6 A man from Maw and Meggins comes to visit Mr. and Mrs. White.

B Read the story excerpt again. Then complete the sentences by circling the correct answer.

1. The word *expectantly* in line 5 means with anger / in anticipation.
2. The word *sorry* in line 31 means in trouble / embarrassed.
3. The word *solemnly* in line 46 means very cheerfully / seriously.
4. The word *consequences* in line 54 means bad or harmful results / positive or exciting results.
5. The phrase *your loss* in line 83 refers to the death of a loved one / something misplaced.

C Pair work. Answer these questions on a separate piece of paper. Then check your answers with a partner.

1. How does Sergeant-Major Morris feel about the monkey's paw?
   What does Herbert think of it? Explain your answers.
2. A man from the factory comes to visit the Whites. How does he feel?
   Why does he feel this way?
3. What is surprising about the end of the story excerpt?

▶ **Ask & Answer**

What is the moral of this story? Explain your answer.
If you were given three wishes, what would you ask for?
How would your life be better? How might it be worse?

> **Inferencing**
>
> Information is not always stated directly. Often a reader must infer, or make guesses about something, using information that is available in the reading.

The Monkey's Paw

Adapted from a story by W. W. Jacobs

Outside, it was a stormy night, but in the White's small living room, the fire burned brightly. Mr. White and his son, Herbert, were playing a game of chess when there was a knock at the door.

5 "There he is," said Herbert expectantly, rising with his father.

Moments later, Mr. White entered the room, followed by a tall, heavy-set man.

"Sergeant-Major Morris," White said, introducing his friend.

10 The middle-aged soldier shook hands with Mrs. White and Herbert. He then chose a comfortable chair by the fire while Mr. White prepared drinks. After his third drink, Morris's eyes got brighter, and he began to tell stories of distant

15 countries. The family listened with interest.

"I'd like to travel myself," said White. Say… what was that you were telling me the other day about a monkey's paw from India, Morris?"

"Nothing," said the soldier quickly. "Anyway,

20 nothing worth hearing."

"Monkey's paw?" said Mrs. White curiously.

"Well," said the sergeant-major, "I guess you could say it's a kind of magic charm…"

25 Morris took the paw out of his pocket and held it up. Mrs. White moved back and frowned; Herbert took it and examined it curiously.

"What's so special about it?" asked Mr. White.

"A holy man in India believed that fate controls

30 our lives. He thought that those who tried to change their fate would be sorry, He put a spell on the paw so that three separate men could each have three wishes."

"And have you had your three wishes?" asked

35 Herbert smiling playfully.

"I have," said the soldier quietly. His face turned white.

"And has anybody else wished?" asked Mrs. White.

40 "The first man had his three wishes, yes. I don't know what the first two were, but the third was for death. That's how I got the paw."

The group fell silent.

Suddenly Morris took the paw and threw it

45 in the fire. Mr. White, with a cry, picked it up.

"Let it burn," said the soldier solemnly.

"If you don't want it, Morris, let me keep it," said Mr. White.

"I won't. I threw it on the fire. Throw it back."

50 White shook his head and looked closely at the paw. "How do you make a wish?" he asked.

Morris sighed. "Hold it in your right hand and wish aloud," he said, "but I'm warning you—there will be consequences."

55 "I don't know what to wish for," said White.

"Wish for two hundred pounds, father," suggested Herbert. He winked at his mother.

His father held up the paw. "I wish for two hundred pounds."

60 Suddenly, White cried out. "It moved! As I made the wish, the paw moved in my hands like a snake!"

"Now dear…" said his wife.

"Well father," said Herbert laughing, "I don't see any money, and I bet I never will."

65 "Very funny," replied White, now calmer. "Still, it scared me all the same."

"I'm sure that Herbert will have some more of his jokes about that monkey's paw when he comes home from work tonight," said Mrs. White, as she and her

70 husband were eating dinner the next evening.

"I'm sure he will," replied Mr. White, "but I'll say it again, the thing moved in my hand."

His wife didn't answer. She was watching a man outside the house. She noticed that the stranger was

75 well dressed. He paused at the gate. Mrs. White hurried to answer the door. She brought the stranger into the room. "I . . . I come from Maw and Meggins," he said nervously.

"The factory? Has something happened to

80 Herbert?" asked Mrs. White, anxiously.

"I'm sorry. Your son was caught in the machinery," the visitor said quietly. "The firm wants me to tell you how sorry they are for your loss," he said. "They wish to give you this check . . ."

85 Mr. White stood up and looked in horror at his visitor. "How much?"

"Two hundred pounds, Sir . . ."

3 WRITING
Chronological order

A Pair work. Read the story. Then answer the questions with a partner.

1. What "mistake" is the author writing about?
2. Why was this a mistake? What went wrong?
3. What is the author's advice to the reader?

Using time expressions and phrases

List events in underlined:chronological order to show when they happened. One way to make the sequence of events clear in a story is to use time expressions and phrases such as the ones below.

First of all,	*Next,*	*Then,*
Two months later,	*Before,*	*After,*
Finally,	*Later,*	

One of the biggest mistakes I've ever made was buying a car. I always wanted a car and thought that having one would make my life easier. I still remember the day I bought the car—my car!—and drove it home. It was the happiest day of my life . . . and then everything went wrong.

First of all, I got a ticket for speeding. I was so excited about driving my new car that I didn't realize how fast I was going. Later, when I got home, there was nowhere to park on the street. I looked for parking for almost thirty minutes. Finally, I found a place—six blocks from my house! The next morning, I decided to drive to school. The traffic was terrible and I was fifteen minutes late for class. All this happened in the first twenty-four hours of owning a car! By the end of the first year, I was almost $2,000 in debt. I needed money for car payments, gas, and insurance. It was crazy! In the end, I had to sell the car to pay my bills.

So what's the moral of the story? If you don't need a car, don't buy one. They are an expensive headache!

B Read the story again and underline the words and phrases used to show the order in which the events happened. The first one has been done for you.

C Think of something you did in your life—something that turned out differently than you expected. List the sequence of events below.

D Use your outline from C and time expressions to write a paragraph about your experience.

E Pair work. Exchange your paper with a partner. Notice the time expressions your partner uses. Is the sequence of events clear? Ask your partner questions about his or her story.

Something you thought would be great: *Example:* buying a dog

- First, of all
- Later
- Finally
- The next morning
- By the end of the first year
- In the end

Activity 1: What's *your* story?

A Imagine that Al Benning (from Listening, page 3) has set up a story booth in your city. You're at the booth with your partner. Read the interview questions below and add two of your own.

Everybody Has a Story

1. Please tell me your name and where you were born.

2. What was it like growing up in _____ [*your city*]? What were some of your favorite places? Have those places changed?

3. What did you want to be when you were a kid?

4. Who were your heroes or role models growing up? Who did you look up to?

5. _____?

6. _____?

B Pair work. Use the questions above to interview your partner.
During the interview, ask additional questions to learn more details. Take notes.

C Group work. Review your notes. What's one new thing you learned about your partner? Tell the class.

Activity 2: The story continues

A Group work. Get into a group of three people. Look back at the end of "The Monkey's Paw" on page 9. Follow the steps below.

1. The story does not end with the Whites receiving the 200 pounds.
   What do you think happens next in the story? Discuss your ideas.
2. Based on your ideas, make up a dialog to end the story.
3. Practice acting out your dialog.

B Group work. Perform your role play for another group. Were your endings similar or different?

 **Check out the CNN® video.** **Practice your English online at** elt.heinle.com/worldpass

Unit 1: What's the Story?

A Match each expression containing *story* with its usage.

1. <u>To make a long story short</u>, I applied for the job, but I didn't get it. _d_
2. I don't care if Laura gets angry with me. I'm not going to her party—<u>end of story</u>. _e_
3. <u>It's the same old story</u>. I went on a diet, I lost ten pounds, and then I gained them all back, just like last time. _c_
4. Patrick's office is neat and well-organized, but his apartment <u>is a different story</u>. _a_
5. <u>What's the story?</u> You promised you'd be here two hours ago! _b_

a. to show a contrast between two things, especially one that surprises you
b. to demand an explanation for something that you are unhappy about
c. to talk about something disappointing that has happened many times before
d. to summarize a sequence of events and avoid telling every detail
e. to put a stop to an argument and show that you don't want to discuss something anymore

B Fill in the blanks with one of the expressions from **A**.

1. I don't care what's on TV! You can't watch it until you've finished your homework. That's the rule—_____.
2. Just like always, I met a nice guy at work, we went out on a few dates, and then he never called me again. _Same old story_.
3. It rained every day, the hotel was terrible, there was a taxi drivers' strike so we couldn't go anywhere—_To make a long story short_, it was an awful vacation.
4. You told me you were going to buy groceries, but the fridge is empty. _____.
5. My old boss was really nice and easygoing. My new boss _is a different story_—he's never satisfied with anything!

C Read about these different types of stories, and think of examples of each.
Then complete the sentences with one of the words in blue, adding articles (*a, an, the*) as needed.

> A **tale** is a story about imaginary events, such as a fairy tale or a folktale. A **report** gives a detailed and objective presentation of facts, such as a newspaper report or a government report, while a **statement** is a short summary of facts. Speakers and writers like to use **anecdotes**, short stories about a real event, to illustrate and explain an idea. A **chronicle** is a long narrative of historical events told in time order. A **yarn** is a long entertaining story loosely based on the truth. Children enjoy **fables**, old stories about animals that teach a moral lesson. And too many people enjoy **gossip**—often untrue rumors about people.

1. Sarah's presentation had some interesting _anecdotes_ about women who have started their own businesses.
2. In my country, we have a lot of old _tales_ about ghosts and princesses.
3. The government issued a brief _report_ about the president's trip to Africa.
4. My grandfather loves to tell _the chronicle_ about his adventures when he was in the navy. He exaggerates a lot, but they're really entertaining!
5. The Ministry of Environmental Protection released _a statement_ on changes in water quality over the past ten years.
6. I don't believe that David is getting married. I think it's just _gossip_.
7. Do you know _the fable_ about the ant and the grasshopper?
8. This history book contains a detailed _a yarn_ of our country's struggle for independence.

Incorrect: *I got on my car and drove to the office.* **Correct:** *I got into my car and drove to the office.*

D Review the meaning of these words from "The Monkey's Paw" on page 9. Then use them to complete the sentences.

> fate (lines 29 & 31) spell (line 31) solemnly (line 46)
>
> expectantly (line 5) consequences (line 54) firm (line 82)

1. My grandmother really believes in _____. She thinks that we can't do anything to change what will happen to us in the future.
2. We waited _____ to find out the winner of the talent competition.
3. Infotek is a _____ that surveys consumers about their opinions on computer products.
4. At the president's funeral, thousands of people lined the streets of the capital and watched _____ as the car carrying his remains passed by.
5. If you cheat on an exam at our university, you face serious _____. You could receive a failing grade, or even be expelled from the university.
6. In the old story, the witch put a _____ on the three children and turned them into trees.

In Other Words

An **alibi** is proof that someone was not near a crime scene and therefore could not have committed the crime: *He is not a suspect because he has a good alibi; he was out of town visiting his sister on the night the robbery took place.*

An **excuse** is a reason given to explain a wrongdoing or offence: *He had a good excuse for being late for the meeting; his car broke down.*

An **explanation** is information given to help someone understand something: *The guide in the museum provided a very clear explanation of how the ancient pottery was made and used.*

A **moral** is the practical lesson in a fable: *The moral of "The Grasshopper and the Ant" is that we should always plan for the future.*

A **lesson** is something that you learn from an experience: *I learned many lessons from traveling alone.* It's also a course of instruction that develops a skill: *Sarah is taking swimming lessons.*

A **message** is the most important idea in a book or movie: *The message of the movie* Titanic *is that love is stronger than death.*

tell and say

The verb *tell* is used with an object:

I told my friend a joke / the truth / a story / a lie / the answer.

We use *say* when we report someone's words:

I said, "You're late."

He said he had missed the bus.

UNIT 2

Technology

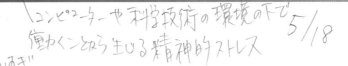

Lesson A | Technostress

コンピューターや科学技術の環境の下で 5/18
働くことにより生じる精神的ストレス

1 VOCABULARY FOCUS

Information <u>overload</u> 過重負担、使いすぎ

 Many people today use IMs (instant messages) to communicate instantly over the
Internet. What are some of the advantages and disadvantages of sending IMs?

分類する。

A Pair work. **Categorize the phrases below. Can you add any more ideas to the list?**

(人・注意を)(～から)そらす   to make easy, covenient

adds stress to the workplace   <u>distracts</u> from regular work   fosters communication
speeds up decision-making   saves time   makes it easier to stay in touch

Advantages of sending IMs	Disadvantages of sending IMs
・a quick way to send a message ・it's easy ・it's convenient → You can do it ・it's free　　　　　from anywhere ・You can send a message and avoid talking	・impersonal 個人の感情を交えない ・it can be habit-forming addictive. ・bad for your eyes?　　癖つきになる ・It's distracting

B Read this letter to an advice columnist. What is Ms. Silva's problem? Notice the words in blue.

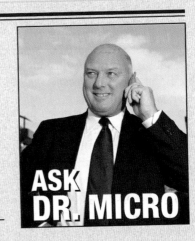

ASK DR. MICRO

Dear Dr. Micro,   ～とかに渡す

I need your help. I am <u>drowning</u> in information overload at work. Between the
telephone calls, voicemail systems, e-mail messages, and faxes, it's becoming too
much. At the office I am often trying to carry on a conversation while typing a
memo and checking the time for my next conference call. 相互作用

I spend my days sitting in front of my computer or talking to clients on the
telephone. I have almost no face-to-face interaction with people during the day.
And at night, it's the same problem as I try to answer e-mail and IMs from my
friends and family. I thought all this technology was supposed to make my life
easier, but it's rapidly becoming a recipe for disaster. I feel chained to my
computer.   秘訣

—*Nadia Silva*

Dear Ms. Silva,

Technology can help us save time and money, but only if we use it wisely. There are some things you can do to help your
situation—it isn't hopeless by any means.   集中、中心   能率的な

reduce

1. Cut back on the multitasking: When you try to do more than one task at once, you lose focus and become less efficient.
2. Spend more time with family, coworkers, and friends: A computer is not a friend—it is an impersonal machine with
   its own limitations. Get out at night and take an exercise class or an art class—something you enjoy. Seeing other
   people promotes a sense of community and besides, it's fun! 座っている
3. Get some exercise: Sitting in front of a computer all day is a sedentary activity—you need to find something active to
   do. Why don't you take time at lunch for a brisk 20-minute walk with a coworker and get caught up on office gossip?

依存
Heavy dependence on computers and other machines can be unhealthy. Follow the suggestions above, though,
and you'll feel freer than you have in a long time. I tried them myself and found them to be liberating indeed. Good luck!
解放する
—*Dr. Micro*

14 Unit 2 • Techonology

C Locate the correct word or phrase in the article on page 14. Write your answers below.

Handwritten margin notes (left):
depend (v.)
~~dependable (adj)~~
~~endance~~ (n.)
enda-
-bility (n.) 動詞変化
~~pendant~~

Find a word or phrase that means:

1. doing more than one thing at once: _multitasking_
2. encourages: _promote_
3. having too much information to absorb: _information overload_
4. reliance on: _dependance_
5. inactive: _sedentary_ 座りがちな

6. contact: _interaction_
7. freeing: _liberating_
8. distant: _impersonal_
9. will likely cause something bad to happen: _recipe for disaster_

Handwritten margin notes (top right):
to rely (v.)
reliable (adj)
reliance (n.) reliant
reliability (n.)

Handwritten note near 9: 適切な

D Pair work. Which of the words or phrases in C can you associate with IMs?

>> **Vocabulary Builder** ▲

A. The word *interaction* is often followed by the preposition *with*. Find the word *recipe* in the column. What preposition is it followed by? What other noun + preposition combinations do you know?

B. Circle the appropriate prepositions.
1. What is the cure (for) / to "technostress?"
2. I haven't had any dealings for / (with) their IT Department.
3. Our dependence (on) / with technology is not always good.

2 LISTENING

When technology doesn't work

Talk about a time you had a problem with technology (for example, your cell phone didn't work). How did you feel? What did you do?

Real English
get to the bottom of (something) = find the truth or cause of a problem

A Listen to this news report. Then circle the correct answers below that describe the report. (CD Tracks 03 & 04)

This is a daytime / (evening) report on radio / (TV) about a (blackout) / storm that happened in the (summer) / winter.

Talking about cause and effect

Speakers use these phrases to link cause and effect:

. . . was the cause of . . .
. . . was responsible for . . .
As a result, . . .

B Listen again. What caused these three things to happen? Write your answers. (CD Track 05)

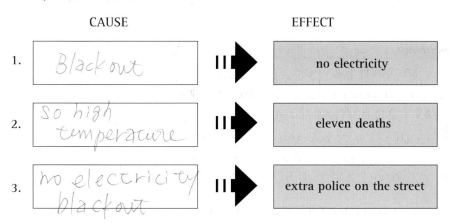

	CAUSE		EFFECT
1.	Blackout	➤	no electricity
2.	So high temperature	➤	eleven deaths
3.	no electricity blackout	➤	extra police on the street

C Listen and complete these items with the appropriate number or numerical expression. (CD Track 06)

a kind of adjective form

1. houses without power: over 100,000
2. length of time with no electricity: 8 hours
3. deaths: 11
4. recent temperatures: well over 100°
5. cooling centers: 12
6. stores broken into: several stores

looting

▶ **Ask & Answer**

Have you ever been in a blackout, a bad storm, an earthquake, or a similar event? What happened?

5/21

---

3 LANGUAGE FOCUS

Review of the passive voice

A Read the sentences. Notice the words in blue.

The object of an active sentence becomes the subject of a passive sentence.

Thomas Edison introduced <u>the first phonograph</u> in 1877.

<u>The first phonograph</u> was introduced in 1877.

Use the passive voice when . . .
- you don't know who did something: Oh no! My bag has been stolen!
- who did the action is not as important as what happened: Our product was tested using the most rigorous standards.   *very strict, carefully*
- who did the action is obvious from the situation: My computer is being repaired today.
- a general group of people do the action: New Year's Day is celebrated here on January 1.

B Pair work. Read these sentences. The passive voice is preferred in each one. Why?
Choose a reason from the chart above. Discuss with a partner.

1. Cell phone usage isn't allowed in the library.
2. Bad news! My shipment is being held at the airport.
3. Has the recycling been picked up yet?
4. Was this product made in Malaysia?

5/26

C Read the ad about the Vesta, a hybrid car, on page 17. Then read these statements below. The statements are incorrect. Respond to each statement with the correct answer. Use the verbs in parentheses and the passive voice.

1. The Vesta uses a single kind of motor.
   <u>No, it doesn't. It's powered by a traditional engine and an electric motor.</u> (power)

2. It's a Japanese car.
   <u>No, it isn't. It's manufactured in Canada.</u> (manufacture)

3. You can only buy it in Canada right now.
   <u>No, you can't. It is also sold in the U.S. and</u> (sell) *Canada.*

4. You can buy it in Europe this week. *or will be ~*
   <u>No, you can't. It has been introduced throughout</u> (introduce) *Latin America and Asia this week.*

5. Critics don't like it. *or was*
   <u>Yes, they do. It has been voted by New Model</u> (vote) *Magazine as "best new car this year."*

6. It's too expensive for the average consumer.
   <u>No, it isn't. It can be purchased by a variety</u> (purchase) *of people.*

☆ *Prius by Toyota*
a hybrid car (gasoline and electricity)

16   Unit 2 • Techonology

Introducing . . . **The Vesta . . .**
made in Canada

+ uses both a traditional engine and an electric motor to save energy
+ already available in the U.S. and Canada
+ available throughout Latin America and Asia this week

Students, doctors, actors, construction workers, artists, housewives . . . join the everyday ranks of Vesta owners! You can afford it!

New Model Magazine voted the Vesta "best new car this year."

D Pair work. Look at the technological achievements to the right. Then ask and answer the questions below with a partner. Use your own ideas to complete the statements. Then make original sentences.

Satellite dish

- Why was . . . invented?
    It was invented so that . . .
    It was invented in order to . . .

- How has the world been changed by this invention?
    The world has become . . .
    Photos can be sent . . .
    TV shows can be watched . . .

E Pair work. What invention in the past fifty years has made the biggest impact on society? Decide on your answer. Take notes on your reasons. Tell the class.

World Link

Wireless technology has brought economic development, increased productivity, and "e-service" opportunities to less-developed and remote areas of the world. For the Ulwazi Project in South Africa, "e-education" programs even let schools "share" teachers via the web using virtual whiteboards and microphones!

Source: *CNN*₀

Digital camera

4 SPEAKING

I'm pretty good at it.

A Pair work. Read about the situation below. Pay attention to the words in blue. Who should Jim go to for help? Why?

Saying you're able or not able to do something

Jim's computer has crashed and he doesn't know what to do. Read what these different people said to Jim.

Paolo: I might be able to help you. I know something about computers.

Kim: Let me look at it. I'm pretty good at fixing things.

Jesse: What should you do? I haven't got a clue about it. Ask Emi.   *idea*

Emi: I know something about computers. I'm busy now, but I can help you later.

Jacques: I'm sorry, but I'm no good at fixing things, especially computers.

Gloria: I don't have the faintest idea how to fix it. Call a repair service.   *very small*

B Read the statements below. What do you notice about the words that follow the expressions in blue?

	Agree	Disagree
1. I might be able to change a tire if I had to.	✓	✓
2. I'm pretty good at typing on an English keyboard.		✓
3. I'm pretty good at golf.		✓
4. I haven't got a clue about scuba diving.	✓	
5. I know something about computers.		✓
6. I'm no good at karaoke.	✓	
7. I'm no good at speaking in front of a group of people.		✓
8. I don't have the faintest idea how to cook Italian food.	✓	

C Pair work. Read the statements in B again. Think about your own answers for each statement, and check (✓) *Agree* or *Disagree*. Then explain your answers to a partner.

> I might be able to change a tire if I had to. My dad showed me how to do it.

> Not me! I wouldn't know what to do!

D Pair work. Is there something your partner knows how to do or is good at that you're not? Ask your partner to explain how to do it.

Technology

Lesson B | Techno-shopping

6/2

1 GET READY TO READ

Shopping habits

6/4

Do you like shopping? Why or why not?
What do you like shopping for?
What do you hate shopping for?

A Pair work. **Complete the shopping survey below. Then explain your answers to a partner.**

SHOPPING SURVEY

1 How often do you go shopping?
○ hardly ever ○ about once a month ○ once a week ○ once a day

almost never
あまり行かない

2 Which sentence best describes your feelings about shopping?
用事
○ It's a chore! If I have to shop, I try to do it quickly.
○ It's OK. I don't mind doing it.
○ I love it! When I shop, I like to take my time and look around.

3 How often do you shop on-line? What do you usually buy?
How often: ○ all the time ○ sometimes ○ rarely ○ never
What: _____

4 Think about the store(s) you go to often. Why do you shop there?
Check all that apply.
○ convenience (store is nearby)   ○ quality products   ○ helpful clerks
○ large selection of products   ○ short checkout lines ○ other _____
○ low prices   ○ interesting, trendy environment

5 Where do you (or your family) do your grocery shopping? Check all that apply.
○ small neighborhood stores   ○ a large supermarket
○ on-line   ○ other _____

6 Do you have a discount or club card* for any store?
○ Yes ○ No

7 How do you usually pay for things?
○ cash ○ debit card ○ check ○ credit card

*Club cards allow entry and offer special discounts at a store.

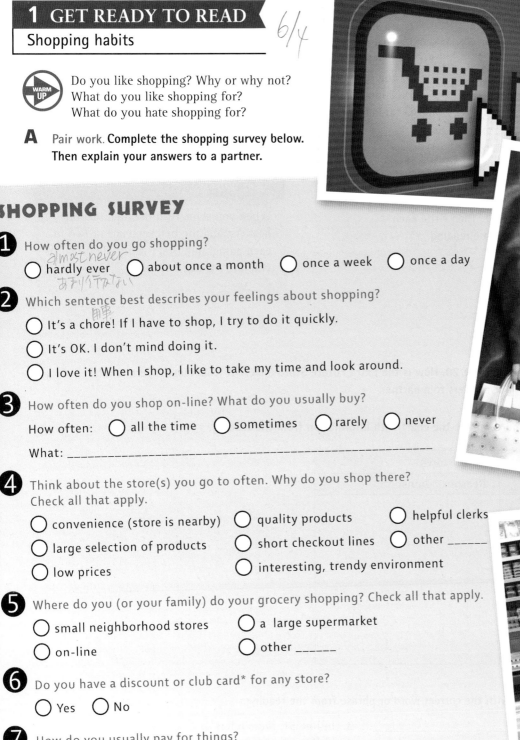

B Pair work. The words in the left column are from the reading on page 21. Match each one with the phrase in the right column that is most similar in meaning. Then check your answers with a partner.

植えつける、たたきこむ

1. display (line 17) _e_   a. a tool or piece of equipment
2. unique (line 25) _h_   b. to implant something into something else
3. device (line 26) _a_   c. to follow, to trace
4. automatically (line 36) _i_   d. in danger, at risk
5. anonymously (line 38) _g_   e. to show publicly
6. embed (line 41) _b_   f. space to yourself so that others cannot see or hear what you're doing
7. track (line 46) _c_   g. namelessly, in secret
8. privacy (line 46) _f_   h. the only one of its kind, special
9. at stake (line 46) _d_   i. done mechanically, without a person doing it
10. benefit (line 49) _j_   j. an advantage

匿名で
はかなし
埋めこむ

2 READING
Not Your Typical Store

A Skim the article quickly on page 21. Then write each heading in the appropriate box in the reading.

How it works
But there are benefits, too . . .
~~A new way to shop~~
So, what's the problem?
A more convenient shopping experience

> Skimming a reading to get the main ideas quickly.
>
> When you skim, read the title, section headers, and the first sentence or two in each paragraph. Don't worry about words you don't know.

B Pair work. Read the article through line 20. How is the Extra Future Store different from most supermarkets? Find three examples. Explain your answers to a partner.

C Read the rest of the article and complete the chart with information from the reading.

Using RFID chips in stores	
Reasons for	**Reasons against**
Shoppers will be able to find items in a store more quickly.	

D Complete the sentences below with the correct word or phrase from the reading.

1. In line 17, *It* refers to _____.
2. In line 41, *them* refers to _____.
3. In line 51, *these* refers to _____.
4. In line 55, *that* refers to _____.

Not Your Typical Store

Brian Nguyen

A new way to shop

It's Tuesday afternoon, and I'm in Rheinburg, Germany (a city just north of Dusseldorf), visiting the Extra Future Store. Metro AG, the parent company of the store, is one of Germany's largest retailers and its "store of the future" is
5 attracting a lot of attention these days—but not for its prices. Instead, people are coming from all over to experience a new way to shop.

The experience is less like shopping in a supermarket and more like playing some kind of high-tech game. It starts as I
10 enter the store and choose a shopping cart. First, I swipe my store ID card through a computer on the cart's handle. The computer's screen comes on, a map of the store appears, and the journey begins.

As I shop, antennas around the store send information
15 about different specials to the computer on my cart. Attracted by one of the ads, I select a jar of olives that are on sale. I hold up the jar to a computer nearby. It displays the price and also suggests that a certain type of Spanish cheese would be good with the olives. The map on my cart shows me where to find
20 the cheese. It's like the store is helping me to shop.

How it works

How does the Extra Future Store make this kind of shopping experience possible? The answer is *radio frequency identification chips* (or RFID, for short). Invented in 1969, RFID chips are about the size of a grain of sand. Each chip
25 has a unique ID number and is attached to a product (e.g., a bottle of olives). Using a wireless device called an "RFID reader," one can get information from a chip about a product—for example, its price and location.

A more convenient shopping experience

This type of technology could mean a more convenient
30 experiece for shoppers. RFID chips will help shoppers find items in a store more quickly—products that are just right for them. In addition, people won't have to wait in long checkout lines to pay. In the supermarket of the future, you will simply walk through a checkout lane. The REID-tagged
35 items in your cart will be read by a scanner, and your credit or debit card will be charged automatically.

So, what's the problems?

Sounds good, right? Not to consumer activist Jeremy Webber. "Right now, I can buy something anonymously, especially if I pay with cash," says Webber. "But today, RFID
40 chips are being put on product packaging. And a growing number of manufacturers are planning to embed them directly into products." (A chip will be sewn into a pair of shoes, for example, or be built into a shampoo bottle.)

"What this means," explains Webber, "is that if the RFID
45 chip isn't disabled before you leave the store, your location could be tracked with an RFID reader. People's privacy is at stake."

But, there are benefits, too?

Megan Lim, a store manager in Australia, believes that Webber's concerns are unnecessary. "Look, there are risks with every kind of new technology. But what about the benefits? If a
50 store uses the chips, it can track which items are popular, and quickly order more of these. Stores can save money by ordering fewer of the less popular items. If the store saves money, then maybe shoppers will pay less for products, too." Lim pauses. "I think a lot of people will be willing to give up some of their
55 privacy for that."

▶ **Ask & Answer**

Would you shop at a place like the Extra Future Store? Why or why not?

3 WRITING

Pros and cons

A Pair work. **In this unit, you read about ways that RFID chips are being used in stores. Read and complete the paragraphs below using the phrases in the box. Then discuss the questions below with a partner.**

> There are also disadvantages   Another drawback   Another benefit
> The downside to this   One advantage is that

[handwritten: One Advantage is that]

Using RFID chips in stores has advantages and disadvantages. (1.) ~~Another drawback~~ shoppers will be able to find items in a store more quickly. A person won't need to wander up and down store aisles looking for products. (2.) *Another benefit* is that shoppers won't have to spend time standing in long checkout lines. They will simply walk through a checkout station, and their credit or debit card will be automatically billed.

(3.) *There are also disadvantages* to using RFID chips in stores, though. As was noted, one of the pluses of using the chips is that a person's account will be automatically billed. (4.) _____, of course, is that a person will need a credit or debit card in order to buy things. (5.) _____ to using RFID chips relates to privacy. Unless a chip is disabled before a shopper leaves the store, his or her location can be tracked.

- How many advantages and disadvantages are discussed in each paragraph?
- Can you think of one more advantage and disadvantage? How would you add these to the paragraphs above?

B Pair work. **Read the ad. With a partner, think of two reasons for and two reasons against using RFID chips on people.**

> ## Call People Trackers Now!
>
> Our company has designed an RFID chip for people.
> The device is embedded under a person's skin.
> You can use it to track:
>
> your spouse, boyfriend or girlfriend,
> your children, or your employees!
>
> For more information, call (800) 555-TRAK today

Advantages	Disadvantages
1. *find where they are now.*	1.
2.	2.

C On a separate piece of paper, write a paragraph describing the pros and cons of using RFID chips with people. Use your ideas from B and the phrases from A in your paragraph.

D Pair work. Exchange your paragraph with a new partner. Notice the phrases your partner uses to describe the advantages and disadvantages.

Activity 1: Technology now and then

A Pair work. How much do you know about technology? Read and discuss the questions with a partner. Try to choose the correct answer for each.

B Group work. Join another pair.

• Compare your answers. Each correct answer is worth 10 points.
• The pair with the most points wins.

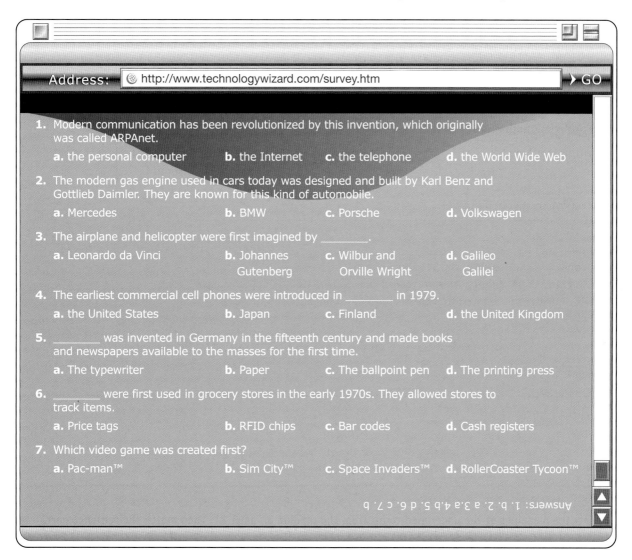

Address: http://www.technologywizard.com/survey.htm → GO

1. Modern communication has been revolutionized by this invention, which originally was called ARPAnet.
   a. the personal computer   b. the Internet   c. the telephone   d. the World Wide Web

2. The modern gas engine used in cars today was designed and built by Karl Benz and Gottlieb Daimler. They are known for this kind of automobile.
   a. Mercedes   b. BMW   c. Porsche   d. Volkswagen

3. The airplane and helicopter were first imagined by _____.
   a. Leonardo da Vinci   b. Johannes Gutenberg   c. Wilbur and Orville Wright   d. Galileo Galilei

4. The earliest commercial cell phones were introduced in _____ in 1979.
   a. the United States   b. Japan   c. Finland   d. the United Kingdom

5. _____ was invented in Germany in the fifteenth century and made books and newspapers available to the masses for the first time.
   a. The typewriter   b. Paper   c. The ballpoint pen   d. The printing press

6. _____ were first used in grocery stores in the early 1970s. They allowed stores to track items.
   a. Price tags   b. RFID chips   c. Bar codes   d. Cash registers

7. Which video game was created first?
   a. Pac-man™   b. Sim City™   c. Space Invaders™   d. RollerCoaster Tycoon™

Answers: 1. b. 2. a 3. a 4. b 5. d 6. c 7. b

Activity 2: The pros and cons

A Pair work. Think of a simple problem in daily life that could be solved with the right technology. What is the problem? What could you invent to solve it?

1. Discuss your ideas.
2. Make a simple drawing of your invention.

B Group work. Take turns presenting your inventions to the rest of the class.

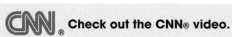 **Check out the CNN® video.** **Practice your English online at** elt.heinle.com/worldpass

Unit 2: Technology

A Some words are frequently used together in a phrase. Read this paragraph and underline the phrases with *trend*.

> Young people in many countries are <u>setting the trend</u> for a new pattern in telecommunication. There is a trend toward having only a cell phone as a replacement for a landline. Experts predict that the current trend will spread to developing countries, and the upward trend in the number of cell phone subscribers will continue for years to come. Analysts theorize that only a few countries will buck the trend and continue to add landlines instead.

B Study the phrases in the box and then complete the sentences with the phrases.

> **Word combinations with *trend***
>
> set(ting) the trend   a trend toward having/buying/making (verb + *ing*)
> the latest/recent/current trend   a trend in communication/fashion/music (noun)
> downward/upward trend   economic/social trends
> reverse/buck the trend

1. In my country, there's _____ getting married at a later age. Nowadays people are waiting until they're 27 or 28.
2. More and more children are overweight. The government is hoping to _____ with nutrition programs and fitness classes in schools.
3. Fewer people every year are using fax machines. This _____ began about ten years ago with the popularity of e-mail.
4. *The Future of Money* is a new book about _____ in the world today.
5. Japanese companies are _____ for energy-efficient hybrid cars.

> **I didn't know that!**
> The English word *robot* comes from a Czech word which means "worker." In 1923, a Czech science fiction writer named Karl Capek wrote a book in which machines take over the world and embed circuits in people's brains to make them work like machines. He called these people *robots*.

C Review the meanings of the underlined terms from the reading on page 21. Then match the sentence parts.

1. I use my <u>debit card</u> ___.
2. I took a <u>shopping cart</u> ___.
3. The <u>checkout lines</u> are very long ___.
4. I have a <u>club card</u> ___.
5. I complained to the <u>manager</u> ___.
6. A special <u>scanner</u> shows you ___.
7. The <u>shelves</u> at the electronics store were empty ___.

a. because I planned to buy a lot of heavy things.
b. after the holiday sale ended.
c. when the store is busy.
d. because a store employee was very rude to me last time.
e. the price and other information about the product.
f. to pay for groceries, gasoline, and things I buy every day.
g. for the music store, so every time I buy ten CDs, I get one free.

Expansion Pages

D The prefix *over–* (meaning "too much") is used with certain nouns, verbs, and adjectives. Match the words with their meanings.

1. overdo it ___
2. overload ___
3. overlook ___
4. overpowering ___
5. overeat ___
6. overdue ___

a. unpleasantly strong
b. not done by the time required
c. give someone too much work or information
d. not notice something
e. eat too much
f. work too hard

E Now complete the sentences with the correct form of the terms in **D**.

1. Be careful not to _____! You just got out of the hospital!
2. All of my bills were _____ last month because I forgot to mail the payments.
3. On holidays, many people tend to _____ at family dinners and company parties.
4. My sister loves to wear perfume, but she uses so much that the scent is almost _____.
5. I had to rewrite my paper for English class. I _____ a lot of spelling mistakes, and my teacher made me correct them.
6. I'm _____ with e-mail messages—I get almost 100 of them every day.

In Other Words

Device is a general word for a machine with a special purpose: *They invented a new device for copying DVDs.*

An appliance is an electrical machine used in the household: *We got all new kitchen appliances, including a stove, fridge, and microwave oven.*

Gadget is an informal word for a small, clever tool: *I bought a gadget that keeps my coffee cup hot on my desk.*

Contraption is a humorous word for a funny-looking machine: *I don't think that contraption will really clean my bathroom automatically.*

Unique means being the only one like this in the world: *The architecture of the Sydney Opera Hall is truly unique.*

One of a kind is an informal expression: *Irina's dress is one of a kind. She made it herself.*

Without equal means better than any other: *The author's knowledge of world history is without equal.*

Special is sometimes used as an informal word for unique: *That photo of my family was a very special gift. Thanks so much!*

 **Watch out!**

unique
Unique is an absolute term and does not have a comparative or superlative form. So you can't say "more unique" or "the most unique." Other words like this are *perfect* and *impossible*.

1 VOCABULARY FOCUS

She's a real go-getter.

What are some characteristics that make someone a good employee?

A Intek Games is looking for a lead designer for their video games division. Read the adjectives below. Then add two that you think are important to the job description on the right.

thorough	motivated	creative
productive	energetic	sincere

B Here are two candidates for the job. Read about each person and notice the words in blue.

INTEK GAMES

Wanted: Lead designer for video games division

- minimum five years experience in the gaming industry
- strong communication and leadership skills
- must be organized
- _____
- _____

Raphael has worked for Intek for six years. He's an early riser, a morning person, and, as a rule, gets to work by 7:00 before anyone else. He works well with other employees and likes collaborating on projects. On the whole, people think of him as a real team player. Even though he's got a great attitude, he can be a hothead under pressure and often loses his temper when there is a deadline. He also ends up doing extra work because he has difficulty saying no when people ask him to do something—even if it isn't his job. This gives him a reputation of being a pushover, although some say it means he's a hard worker who gives 100% to get the project done.

Damita has worked for Intek for five years. She's a real go-getter—a very ambitious employee. She was hired as the receptionist, took some classes, and has worked her way up quickly to be part of the design team. Not only is she a self-starter, she's a real risk taker. She likes to try new ways of doing things, even if it means making mistakes sometimes. Typically, she works a lot harder than she has to. Some of her colleagues say she's an overachiever. She is also a bit of a control freak. She has to have things done her way and often tries to manage even the smallest details of a project. It's very important to her to do a good job, but her colleagues think she tries to do it all and doesn't give them a chance to get their work done at their own pace.

C Pair work. **Read the sentences. Who does each one describe?**
Circle the correct answer. Then compare your answers with a partner.

This person . . .

1.	gets up early.	Raphael	Damita
2.	gets angry easily.	Raphael	Damita
3.	is easily controlled by others.	Raphael	Damita
4.	is a very ambitious person.	Raphael	Damita
5.	likes to give orders.	Raphael	Damita
6.	tries to cooperate with other people.	Raphael	Damita
7.	likes to try new things and isn't afraid of danger.	Raphael	Damita
8.	works harder than necessary to succeed.	Raphael	Damita

>> Vocabulary Builder

Look at these compound nouns and discuss the questions with a partner.

team player   go-getter   overachiever

1. What do you think these words mean?
2. What do you notice about how these words are written?
3. Find other words in the description of Raphael and Damita in
   A that are formed the same way.

▶ **Ask & *Answer***
Which person would
you choose for the
job—Raphael or
Damita? Why?

2 LISTENING
Opposites attract.

A Look at the photos of Sandra and Ali and then
at the words below. Predict which words could
be used to describe each of them.

homebody   free spirit
heartbreaker   night owl
early riser

Sandra

Ali

B Listen to Ali talk about a problem he's having with Sandra. What is the problem?
Write your answer below. (CD Tracks 07 & 08)

_____

_____

C Listen and write down the key words that describe each personality type.
Then circle the person each describes. (CD Track 09)

Personality type	Key words	Name	
1. a homebody	stays at home	Ali	Sandra
2. a free spirit		Ali	Sandra
3. a heartbreaker		Ali	Sandra
4. a night owl		Ali	Sandra

▶ **Ask & *Answer***
Which of the words in A describe
you or someone you know? In what
other situations do people have to
compromise to make things work?

3 LANGUAGE FOCUS

Adverb clauses of contrast, purpose, and time

Adverb Clauses

An adverb clause tells why, when, how, or where something happened. It modifies the verb or the main clause in a sentence.

A Read these sentences. Underline the adverb clause in each sentence.
Circle the word or phrase that introduces the clause.
Then answer the questions that follow.

Set 1   a. I left the party early because I wasn't feeling well.
b. I studied Italian so that I could communicate with my relatives. *a*
c. Since the movie doesn't start until 9:00, why don't we have dinner now?

Set 2   a. I jumped when I heard a loud noise. *c*
b. Whenever I'm at home, I like to relax and just do nothing.

Set 3   a. Though it was hot and humid, I didn't mind. *b*
b. I look a lot like my father, although he doesn't wear glasses and I do. *b*

Which set of sentences contains adverb clauses that express:
a. a reason or purpose for doing something? __1__
b. opposition or contrast? __3__
c. time? __2__

Real English
You can use *even though* instead of *although* or *though* with no change in meaning.

B Circle the correct word or phrase to complete each sentence.

1. (Even though / Because) I'm a morning person, I often arrive at school by 7:00 A.M.
2. (Since / Though) everyone's opinion is important, I consult with others before I make a big decision.
3. I get angry (whenever / even though) I make a mistake.
4. I like to supervise projects (although / so that) everything runs smoothly.
5. (Even though / Since) I don't consider myself ambitious, it's true that I never give up.
6. You have to take risks (since / though) you only live once.
7. I don't like to be in charge (so that / because) no one listens to me.
8. (Although / Since) everyone tells me not to work so hard, I can't stop myself.

~を預って、~の担任の、

C Pair work. What kind of person do you think would say each
sentence in B? Which sentences might you say?

> I think an early riser would say the first sentence.

> I definitely wouldn't say it because I like to sleep late!

D Complete each sentence with a logical ending.
Compare your answers with a partner.

1. Even though it was raining and cold, we decided to _____.
2. Because he's an overachiever, he always _____.
3. Since our plane leaves at 7:00 A.M., why don't we _____?
4. Although he seems like a team player, _____.
5. She took some web design classes so that _____.
6. She exercises and eats well because she _____.

E Pair work. **Complete these sentences with your own information. Then share your information with a partner.**

1. I always take _____
   whenever _____.
2. I hardly ever _____ because _____
   _____.
3. I'm studying English so that _____
   _____.
4. Although I didn't _____, _____
   _____.

> I always take my laptop whenever I go on vacation. What about you?

F Pair work. **Read the situation below. Look at the list of advantages and disadvantages and add one or two of your own ideas to each list. Then, create a role play in which you discuss the possibilities, and then decide what to do. Use adverb clauses in some of your responses.**

Scott and Zach are roommates. Doug is looking for a room. Play the roles of Scott, who wants another roommate and Zach, who doesn't.

Advantages of getting a roommate	Disadvantages of getting a roommate
The rent will be cheaper. Doug's a very neat person. He's an early-riser who's rarely home. _____ _____	The apartment will be more crowded. Doug has two cats. He's quiet, but his friends aren't. _____ _____

Scott: I think we should get a roommate. The rent will be cheaper.
Zach: I don't know. Even though we can save money, the apartment will be more crowded.
Scott: That's true, but think about the chores. Since Doug's a neat person, . . .

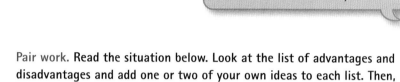
World Link

"Ketsuekigata," the study of blood types and personality, is so important in Japan that when Naoko Takeuchi wrote the character profiles for her hit cartoon series *Sailor Moon*, she included the characters' blood types along with their names, hobbies, and favorite foods. (In case you're wondering, Sailor Moon is a Type O.)

4 SPEAKING

In general, what do you like to do for fun?

A Look at the sentences in the box. Pay attention to the words in blue. Are the conversations about things that happen all of the time or most of the time?

Making general statements

What kind of music do you listen to?
> Generally speaking, I prefer rock. I sometimes also listen to R&B.

In general, what do you like to do for fun?
> I enjoy listening to music and shopping.

Where do you like to go out with your friends?
> For the most part, I like to go to clubs.

Typically, what do you do on the weekend?
> I sleep late!

What do you do when you face a difficult problem?
> As a rule, I think it over first. If I can't solve the problem, I'll ask a friend for advice.

How often do you study?
> Normally I study everyday after school.

B Pair work. Answer the questions.

1. How would you answer the questions in the box above?
2. Add three questions of your own. Practice with a partner.
3. Based on your partner's answers, what do you think his or her personality type is?

C Group work. Work with another pair. Take turns describing your partner's personality type. Use the phrases in the box in A to explain your conclusions.

> *Generally speaking, my partner is a free spirit. She likes to relax on the weekends, go clubbing, and have fun.*

D Pair work. Role-play the following situation. Before you begin, choose one of the personality types below, but don't tell your partner. During the role play, answer the questions based on the personality type you choose.

free spirit	hot head	overachiever	risk taker
go-getter	introvert	pushover	team player

Situation: You're at the airport. Your flight has been delayed for two hours. You talk with each other while you are waiting for your flight. Take turns asking each other questions about your jobs, your hobbies, how you spend your free time, and so on.

E Pair work. Follow the steps below.

1. Guess your partner's personality type.
2. Change personality types and repeat the role play.

Personality

| *Lesson B* | What type are you? |

1 GET READY TO READ

Describing character

6/24

WARM UP What kind of personality do you have?
How about your friends? Your family?

A Pair work. There are many different ways to assess personality. Which ways below are you familiar with? What do you know about them? Discuss it with a partner.

astrology   blood type   numerology   palm reading

> **Using prefixes and suffixes**
>
> To guess the meaning of new words pay attention to prefixes, suffixes, and familiar parts of the word (e.g., *drive* in the word *driven*).

B Pair work. Study the personality adjectives in blue. Circle the word on the right that has the same or a similar meaning. Check your answers with a partner.

1. peaceful *b*   a. nervous   b. calm
2. driven *a*   a. ambitious   b. lazy
3. easygoing *b*   a. strict   b. relaxed
4. assertive *a*   a. direct   b. shy
5. unpredictable *b* a. expected   b. changeable

6. optimistic *b*   a. negative   b. positive
7. nurturing *a*   a. comforting   b. upsetting
8. systematic *b*   a. messy   b. orderly
9. refined *a*   a. well-mannered   b. impolite
10. introspective *b* a. shallow   b. thoughtful

C Pair work. Before you take the quiz on page 32, read the passage that follow. Then discuss the questions below with a partner.

1. According to this passage, where does the idea of "the five elements" come from?
2. What are the five elements and where do they exist?
3. What happens if the five elements are not in balance?

The Five Elements

Traditional Chinese medicine teaches us that there is a set of five elements, or five kinds of energy: wood, water, metal, fire, and earth. They exist everywhere and in everyone. Our feelings and personality and even our body can be described using the five elements. People who work with the five elements think it is important to keep these energies in balance in order to maintain harmony and happiness in our life. If we have too much of one element or not enough of another, trouble may occur.

A Answer questions 1–4 below. Check as many items as apply.

Spotlight on . . . Personality

1. Which word(s) describe you?

☐ assertive   ☑ easygoing   ☐ nurturing   ☐ peaceful   ☐ systematic

☐ driven   ☐ introspective   ☐ optimistic   ☐ refined   ☐ unpredictable

2. Which color(s) do you like?

☐ black   ☐ green   ☐ red   ☐ yellow   ☑ white

3. Which type(s) of food do you usually eat?

☐ bitter (leafy green vegetables)   ☐ spicy   ☑ salty   ☐ sweet

☐ sour (citrus fruits, pickled vegetables)

4. Which season(s) do you look forward to?

☐ winter   ☐ spring   ☐ summer   ☑ autumn

Score

Water _____   Wood _____   Fire _____   Earth _____   Metal _____

B Now read the description of each element on page 33. As you read, circle the words you checked in A. Then write the number of circled words for each element in the *Score* section.

C Read the article again. Find these facts in the reading.

According to the passage, which element is associated with . . .

1. a caring and nurturing parent? _____
2. peaceful thought and saving energy? _____
3. great energy and powerful emotions? _____
4. a time of choosing the most important things? _____
5. new beginnings and growth? _____
6. time alone? _____
7. being a risk taker? _____
8. decorating one's surroundings? _____
9. perfectionism? _____
10. spaciousness and simplicity? _____

D Pair work. Find one negative personality adjective that describes each element in the reading. What does each adjective mean? Compare your answers with a partner.

Water _____   Fire _____   Metal _____

Wood _____   Earth _____

Understanding the Five Elements

The passage below describes each element in detail, and outlines the effects each has on an individual's personality and behavior.

WATER 水

This element is represented by the color black and the calm stillness of winter. Like this season, water energy is associated with quiet reflection and the conservation and storage of energy and strength.

People whose dominant element is water have a preference for salty foods. They tend to be peaceful and introspective, though they can also be stubborn individuals who resist change. Water people value privacy and rarely share their personal thoughts and feelings with others.

Individuals with very little water often lack good sense. They tend to have a difficult time making decisions and often give up easily.

WOOD 木

This element is represented by the color green and the rebirth of spring. Wood energy is associated with youth, expansion, and the making of future plans and decisions.

People whose dominant element is wood have a preference for sour foods. They tend to be driven, assertive individuals, which can sometimes make them argumentative and difficult to get along with. Wood people are idealists who believe that there is a "right way" of doing things. However, they can also be understanding, helpful individuals who are happy to assist others in need.

Those with little or no wood tend to have a difficult time forming their own opinions and are easily persuaded by others.

FIRE 火

Not surprisingly, this element corresponds to the color red and the season of summer. Fire energy is associated with openness and abundance as well as with strong emotions such as love and joy.

People whose dominant element is fire have a preference for bitter foods. They tend to be optimistic, energetic, unpredictable individuals. Fire people often have strong opinions, and are, by nature, risk takers: they are passionate people who love excitement and change. Like fire, though, they can also be destructive and may hurt or offend others with their short tempers.

People with little or no fire tend to worry a lot and have very little self-confidence.

EARTH 土

This element is represented by the color yellow and is related to late summer—a time of wellbeing when all things are in balance.

People whose dominant element is earth have a preference for sweet foods. Earth people enjoy collecting things and decorating their surroundings. They are slow to change their minds and rarely lose their tempers. Like "Mother Earth" they project an image of comfort and stability. Earth people tend to be easygoing, caring, and nurturing, although like some parents, they can also be overprotective.

People who lack earth tend to ignore others' advices and opinions and will frequently break their promises.

METAL 金

This element is represented by the color white and is related to the season of autumn—the time when we select the essentials, and let go of waste in preparation for winter.

People whose dominant element is metal have a preference for spicy foods. They tend to be systematic and refined, but are sometimes viewed by others as somewhat distant or aloof. Metal people work best in disciplined, organized environments. They like wide, open spaces, and prefer simplicity in their surroundings. Too much clutter or decoration makes a metal person uncomfortable.

Individuals who lack metal tend to have a difficult time making quick decisions and expressing their true feelings.

▶ **Ask & Answer**

Which element(s) are dominant in your personality (i.e., have higher scores)?
Which element(s) do you have very little of (have lower scores)?
Do you agree with the description of your personality? Why or why not?

3 WRITING
Describing a location

A Pair work. Read the paragraph below. Then look around the room you're in now.
What are three things you would change? Compare your answers with a partner.

    In this unit, you read that it's important to keep the five elements in balance to create harmony in your life. This theory can also be applied to many things—including decorating a home or an office. In fact, some people believe that the atmosphere of a place—the lighting, the arrangement of furniture, the color, the temperature, and the plants—can all make a big difference.

B Think of an indoor location (a café, a bedroom, a club) you like. What are the features of the place that make it feel good to be there? Include the lighting, the furniture, the colors, the smells, and so on. List the features here.

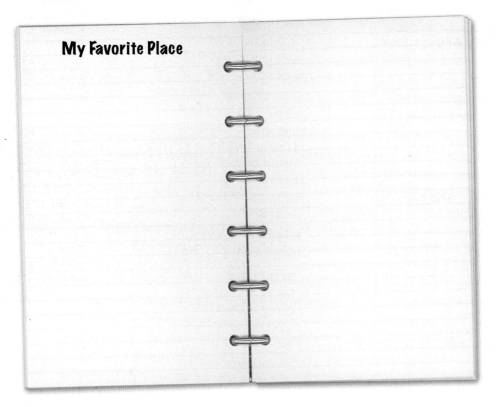

My Favorite Place

C Write a paragraph about the place in B. Begin your paragraph with a topic sentence and use the words and phrases below to organize your paragraph.

Topic sentence: There are several reasons why _____ is my favorite place.

> First of all, . . .   In addition, . . .
> Another reason is . . .   Finally, . . .

There are several reasons why The Crystal Café is my favorite place. First of all, the café has big windows, so it's always well-lit. Another reason is . . .

D Pair work. Read your partner's paragraph. Ask your partner about details that aren't clear to you. Answer the questions below.

1. What does the paragraph tell you about your partner's personality?
2. How do your favorite places compare? Are they similar or very different?

Activity 1: Who do we vote off?

A Read the information below about a reality show.

A new reality TV show follows Noel Barnes and the staff of Blow Dry, a trendy hair salon in Beverly Hills, California through the first year of business. Noel Barnes opened the salon a year ago and currently employs four people. On tonight's show, Noel needs to save money and is going to have to let one of his employees go. Who should it be and why?

About her: She is a driven go-getter. Many of her clients are well-known celebrities. She often argues with Noel about how to run the salon. She gossips a lot with clients about other clients.

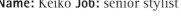
Name: Keiko **Job:** senior stylist

About him: He is a friend of Noel's. He is a friendly team player who gets along well with everyone. He is new and isn't bringing much money into the salon. He has a good rapport with clients and is very professional.

Name: Drew **Job:** stylist

About her: She is a hardworking self-starter who manages the day-to-day operations of the salon. Her father is a major investor in Blow Dry. She is friendly with customers, but perhaps talks too much.

Name: Yasmin **Job:** Noel's assistant

About him: He is Blow Dry's most popular stylist. Although he sometimes is rude, clients come from far away to have him cut their hair. He is a bit of a troublemaker. He has an unpredictable temper. He gives great haircuts.

Name: Jon **Job:** stylist

B Group work. Discuss the following questions. Explain your answers to the class.

1. Who should Noel let go?
2. Why that person and not one of the others?

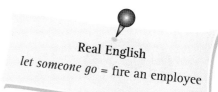
Real English
let someone go = fire an employee

Activity 2: He's a bit of a shy person . . .

With a partner, take turns playing this game.

1. Choose one item each from Group A and B.
2. Make sentences about yourself or someone you know. Explain your answers.
3. Cross off each square in your chart as you use it.

My friend Pat is a bit of a shy person. For example . . .

Group A			Group B		
a really	a complete	such	friendly salon	talkative	a pushover
a bit	so	a bit of	a shy person	homebody	lazy

  Check out the CNN® video.   **Practice your English online at** elt.heinle.com/worldpass

Unit 3: Personality

A Study the phrases in the box and think of examples from your own life. Then use the phrases to complete the sentences below.

> **Word combinations with *personality***
>
> *a strong personality* = a person who is forceful or aggressive
> *a split personality* = a person who has two opposite characteristics
> *a personality clash* = a disagreement between people who are very different
> *a personality disorder* = a psychological illness
> *a personality trait* = a characteristic
> *a TV/radio/sports personality* = a celebrity

1. My best friend really has _____. At work, he's very aggressive, but he's a real pushover with his family.
2. I had to leave my job because of _____ with my boss. She was a real control freak who disagreed with practically everything I did.
3. Nathan's brother is _____. He played on the national soccer team, and now he's a well-known coach.
4. A person who has _____ is often driven and assertive.
5. _____ is a kind of disease.
6. Being lazy and messy are two _____ that I really dislike.

B Match the antonyms for personality. Then circle the ones that describe you!

1. optimistic ____	6. systematic ____	a. flexible	f. disorganized
2. messy ____	7. shallow ____	b. driven	g. rude
3. nervous ____	8. argumentative ____	c. friendly	h. agreeable
4. well-mannered ____	9. lazy ____	d. calm	i. introspective
5. stubborn ____	10. aloof ____	e. organized	j. pessimistic

Incorrect: *Would you like to join us in a cup of coffee?*   **Correct:** *Would you like to join us for a cup of coffee?*

C Complete the sentences with the noun that has a meaning related to the underlined adjective.

> control freak   overachiever
> hothead   pushover

1. My boss is totally <u>driven</u>. I'd say she's a real _____.
2. Jun-Ho is very <u>easy-going</u>. In fact, he's a total _____.
3. My brother is very <u>unpredictable</u> and gets angry easily. He's a real _____.
4. Dr. Sanchez is a little bit too <u>systematic</u>. Frankly, I'd have to say he's a real _____.

D Circle one word in each set that doesn't fit. Use your dictionary as necessary.

1. peaceful	easygoing	calm	driven
2. harmony	conflict	peace	stillness
3. extrovert	privacy	introspective	personal
4. salty	loud	sour	bitter
5. aloof	assertive	aggressive	argumentative
6. optimistic	joyful	gloomy	cheerful
7. risk-taker	cautious	unpredictable	passionate
8. contentment	well-being	disappointment	satisfaction

E Read the first sentence and pay attention to the word in bold.
Then circle the word in parentheses that best completes its meaning.

1. In my opinion, Jack is completely **unreliable**. You (can / shouldn't) rely on him for anything.
2. My parents were **overprotective** when I was a child. They (seldom / always) let me try risky things.
3. Dale is a very **thoughtful** person. He thinks (a lot / very little) about other people.
4. I had a very **uncaring** teacher last year. She really (was / wasn't) concerned about her students' success.
5. Government employees need to be more **cooperative**. They need to work (alone / together) for the good of the country.
6. Don't be so **careless**! You really have to (pay more attention / stop worrying).

In Other Words

An ambitious person has a strong desire to be successful: *Vera is really ambitious about becoming a physicist and winning the Nobel Prize!*
If someone is motivated, he or she has strong reasons for doing something: *Jun-Ho is motivated to improve his English because he's moving to Canada next month.*
Determined means not letting anyone stop you: *The team was determined to win the championship game.*
Pushy (informal) refers to someone who is unpleasantly aggressive in getting what they want: *That car salesman was really pushy about trying to sell me an SUV.*

Describe means to tell what something is like: *She described her hometown / the ceremony / his personality.*
Explain means to make something clear and easy to understand: *He explained the reasons / the situation / how to use the machine.*
Portray means to describe according to one's own view: *The movie portrayed doctors as greedy and uncaring.*

relationship adverbs
Use only one adverb in each sentence to show the relationship between clauses.
> *She's my best friend, <u>so</u> I understand her problems.*
> <u>Because</u> *she's my best friend, I understand her problems.*
> ~~<u>Because</u> *she's my best friend, so I understand her problems.*~~

Expansion Pages

Review: Units 1–3

1 LANGUAGE CHECK

There is a mistake in the underlined part of each sentence. Rewrite each underlined section correctly. One sentence has no mistakes. Write OK next to it.

1. All tourists entering our country <u>has to be checked</u> for the proper visa. _____have to be checked_____
2. Do you know whether the computer <u>has repaired yet</u>? _____
3. I like to go to bed early <u>although I'll</u> feel well rested the next day. _____
4. I traveled in Southeast Asia last year, but <u>I've never went</u> to China. _____
5. My parents and <u>I lived in the same house</u> since 1989. _____
6. I think Mi-Ran <u>has graduated from</u> Seoul National University two years ago. _____
7. Hybrid cars <u>can be buy</u> in a limited number of countries so far. _____
8. <u>Though my job interview</u> is tomorrow at 8 A.M., I think I should catch the bus at 7:15. _____
9. <u>Rita has goes</u> on a diet every year on January 1, but she never loses any weight. _____
10. What has been the most interesting topic <u>that we were studied</u>? _____
11. Whenever we <u>go for vacation</u>, we like to plan everything in advance. _____
12. People <u>are sometimes surprising</u> to learn that TV was invented in 1927. _____
13. In 1999, <u>I've quit my job</u> in London and moved to Brussels. _____
14. <u>Even though I forget</u> her birthday every year, my girlfriend still loves me. _____
15. Radioactivity <u>was discovered from</u> Marie Curie in the nineteenth century. _____

2 VOCABULARY CHECK

Read the article and use the word in parentheses to form a new word or phrase to complete the sentence.

I read a really interesting article by a woman named Brenda Gaines—it's the (1. cover) _____cover story_____ in *Business 2000* magazine this week. She's a reporter for the magazine, and to (2. piece) _____ a story explaining the poor customer service at a cell phone company, she secretly got a job as a representative and worked there for a month.

Ms. Gaines said it almost ruined her life. For one thing, she had to start work at 6 A.M., and she's never been (3. rise) _____. All day, she was completely overloaded with work. She had only two minutes to deal with each phone call, even if the customer had a complicated problem. She said that didn't give her enough time for (4. act) _____ with the callers. The job involved constant (5. task) _____—she had to answer her phone, fill out forms, and respond to e-mail, often all at the same time.

When she first started the assignment, she says she was a real (6. get) _____, and truly wanted to help the customers. But some of them were terrible (7. hot) _____ who shouted and even cursed at her. And her supervisor sounded like a complete (8. control) _____—he even recorded how much time each employee spent in the bathroom! Gaines was finally fired from her job after a month because they said she wasn't a (9. play) _____ and didn't work well with her colleagues.

Gaines's story is easy to believe—you can't (10. make) _____ details like that. And she made an important point. Cell phone companies need to end their (11. heavy) _____ on undertrained, badly paid workers. There is too much (12. at) _____. If customers receive poor service, they will take their business elsewhere.

3 NOW YOU'RE TALKING!

Situation 2

Situation 3

A Day in the Life of ...

A Pair work. Choose one of the pictures and imagine yourselves in the situation. What would the people talk about? Briefly review the language notes from Units 1–3.

B Pair work. Read the statements in C and add two of your own goals. Then role-play the situation you chose keeping your speaking goals in mind.

C Now rate your speaking. Use + for good, ✓ for OK, and − for things you need to improve.

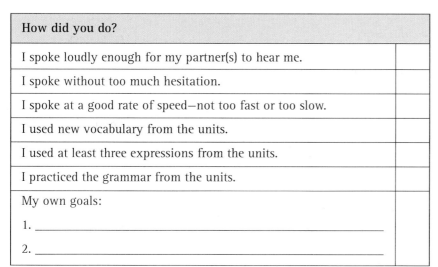

How did you do?	
I spoke loudly enough for my partner(s) to hear me.	
I spoke without too much hesitation.	
I spoke at a good rate of speed—not too fast or too slow.	
I used new vocabulary from the units.	
I used at least three expressions from the units.	
I practiced the grammar from the units.	
My own goals: 1. _____ 2. _____	

Make an Impact

Lesson A | Change your world

1 VOCABULARY FOCUS
Generational differences

 WARM UP What three words would you use to describe your friends and others of your generation? An older generation?

A Pair work. These words and phrases are used in the reading below. Circle the ones that are familiar to you. Look at the roots of the unfamiliar words. With a partner, can you guess their meanings?

visionary	escapist	activist	motivated	circumstances
be aware of	generation	issues	tradition	apathetic

B Read each opinion and complete the statement that follows.

Gary

Where are all the young visionaries—the people who want to make a difference in the world? It seems that most of the younger generation are so escapist: they're too busy watching TV, playing video games, and making money to care about the issues facing the world. Instead of "slacking off," they could be making a difference. Back in the sixties and seventies we were activists: we marched and protested to change our world. Who is going to carry on this tradition of activism?

He thinks _____.

The people of my generation are not slackers! Many of us are motivated and care about what's happening in the world—we're not as apathetic as you make us sound. We're very aware of the problems in the world today and know that we have a role to play in creating a positive future. But our circumstances are different from yours, so don't expect us to do things the same way.

She thinks _____.

Briana

C Circle the correct answers.

1. A **visionary** has positive ideas about the past / future.
2. People in the same **generation** are roughly the same age / personality type.
3. An **escapist** thinks a lot about real / imaginary life.
4. An **issue** is an important problem or subject / conversation that people are discussing.
5. An **activist** works for / avoids social or political change.
6. To **carry on a tradition** means to stop / continue doing something from the past.

7. A **motivated** person is determined / unsure about something.
8. An **apathetic** person is uninterested in / curious about everything.
9. To **be aware of** something is to know / guess that something exists or is happening.
10. The **circumstances** of your life are the overall factors / people that influence your life.

Vocabulary Builder ▲

The prefix *a* in the word *apathetic* means "not" or "without."
Read each sentence below and paraphrase it.

1. Julio was <u>apolitical</u>.   <u>Julio wasn't interested in politics</u>   .
2. Cats are <u>asocial</u> animals. _____
3. These days, it's <u>atypical</u> to have more than two children.

   _____

4. He's a completely <u>amoral</u> person.

   _____

2 LISTENING

A summer internship

If you could do an internship, what kind of organization would you like to work for? What would you like to learn about as an intern?

Real English
An *internship* is a short-term, supervised work experience related to a student's major program and/or career plans.

A Read this ad about an internship opportunity.
Then listen and answer the questions. (CD Tracks 10 & 11)

1. Where do you think this conversation is taking place?

   _____

2. Who is Samir? _____
3. Who is Jeff? _____
4. Who is Marcie? _____

Intern for the summer at the Foundation for Global Issues (FGI) Wanted: Intelligent, outgoing individual to work in our office. Must be self-motivated and have good writing/speaking/listening skills. Computer friendly and good with numbers helpful. Unique opportunity to learn about global activism.

B Listen again. What will Samir be doing?
Complete the list. (CD Track 12)

1. attending   <u>meetings with government officials and their staff</u>
2. taking   _____
3. writing   _____
4. analyzing   _____
5. updating   _____

C Pair work. Look back at the ad in A. How do the qualities that FGI is looking for relate to Samir's job responsibilities?

FGI is looking for someone with good writing skills. Samir will be taking notes during important meetings.

▶**Ask & Answer**
Does Samir's internship sound interesting to you? Do you think it's a job you could do? Why or why not?

D Based on what you know about Samir's internship, which tasks do you think he might work on in the future? Check (✓) the boxes.

- [ ] measuring the difference in world population between five years ago and today
- [ ] hiring new staff for the office
- [ ] creating a new web site for FGI
- [ ] leading a meeting with government officials
- [ ] writing the announcement of a new FGI program

Modals and phrasal modals

A Pair work. **Read what Ana wrote about her family's effort to conserve water. Circle the best answer for each item. Check answers with a partner.**

Last summer, it hardly rained. During that time, water use was restricted and we (1. weren't allowed to / weren't required to) water our lawns during the day. My family (2. should have / may have) followed that law, but we didn't and we (3. were able to / had to) pay a fine to the city. Our family (4. has to / had to) change our regular routines after that. We became more aware of the whole issue of water use, and ways to cut back. First, you (5. should / shouldn't) leave the water running when brushing your teeth. It doesn't seem like a lot of water, but every drop adds up. Second, although we all (6. have to / don't have to) drink a lot of water every day to stay healthy, we (7. should / shouldn't) buy bottled water because sometimes we just want a sip or two, and the rest goes into the trash. Third, reuse the towels when you stay in a hotel more than one night. You (8. have to / don't have to) have a clean towel every day. I became aware that each one of us (9. can / should) make a difference with a little effort. By the end of the summer, our family (10. is permitted to / was permitted to) water our lawn again. We're still motivated to keep up our new habits, though.

B Complete the chart below with an appropriate modal or modal phrase. Use the information in A to help you.

Present	Past
ability can am/is/are able to	ability could was/were able to
giving permission can/may am/is/are permitted to am/is/are allowed to	giving permission could was/were permitted to was/were allowed to
necessity must have to am/is/are required to	necessity had to was/were required to
lack of necessity don't/doesn't have to	lack of necessity didn't have to
advice should shouldn't	advice/regret should have shouldn't have

C Pair work. Use the chart in B to complete the conversations below. Use the affirmative or negative form. More than one answer may be possible. Compare your answers with a partner.

1. A: I'm graduating next year and don't know what to do next.
   B: In my opinion, you _____should_____ go to college. Otherwise, how will you get a good job?

2. A: How was the exhibit at the art museum?
   B: Great! Best of all, it was free! I _____shouldn't / didn't have to_____ pay a thing.

3. A: Who did you support in the last election?
   B: I _____didn't_____ vote then. I was too young at the time. couldn't

4. A: It's impossible to change anything in the world.
   B: That's not true. You _____can_____ make a difference. You just _____should / have to_____ get involved first.

5. A: He _____should have_____ completed his job application by Monday, but he didn't.
   B: He's so apathetic. He doesn't seem to care about anything.

6. A: Why _____should_____ we hire you for this internship?
   B: Well, for one thing I _____am able to / can_____ talk about the issues. I'm very well informed.

7. A: _____Can_____ I call you to discuss this tomorrow?
   B: I'm sorry, but I _____can_____ do it tomorrow. How about Friday?

8. A: How's work going? Did you _____have to_____ work overtime to make your deadline last week?
   B: Yeah, I did. But, I _____didn't have to_____ go to work on Thursday or Friday this week, so I'm happy.

D Group work.
Read about this job opportunity aboard the Peace Boat. Then follow the steps below.

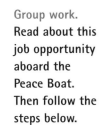

CLASSIFIED JOBS March 18

ACTIVITIES COORDINATOR

We are currently accepting applications for Activities Coordinator on the Peace Boat, an international non-profit organization that travels throughout the world from Japan on "peace voyages." Participants visit different countries and meet local people to promote peace, human rights, and respect for the environment.

The Coordinator can join Peace Boat participants in all activities on shore. The Coordinator will interview with us, but it is not necessary to come to Tokyo to do so. All expenses will be covered for the trip, but the Coordinator is responsible for obtaining a passport and proper immunizations. Without these, the Coordinator cannot board the ship.

Job requirements: speak some English; ability to prepare students on board for cultural exchange activities with locals (such as soccer games, mural painting, and tree planting). Preferred but not necessary: speak some Spanish and Japanese; experience in teaching sports and art.

1. Discuss the job requirements for the Activities Coordinator by completing these sentences:

a. The candidate has to . . .
b. He or she is required to . . .
c. He or she absolutely must . . .
d. He or she doesn't have to . . .
e. It's OK if the Coordinator can't . . .
f. The Coordinator is permitted to . . .

2. Do you think you'd be right for the job? Why or why not? Tell your group.

4 SPEAKING

I hate to disagree with you, but . . .

A Pair work. Read the two conversations. What is the relationship between the speakers in each one?

Conversation 1

Ginny: I really think we need to cut out the kids' computer classes. Between that and soccer practice, they have no free time at all after school.

Doug: I'm not so sure about that. They're in middle school now, and they need to know about computers.

Ginny: Oh, come on! They were still doing homework at 10:00 last night.

Doug: Really? Well, you may be right about the lessons, then. Kids need time to just play.

Conversation 2

Mr. Yuan: The way I see it, what we need is an advertising campaign that will shock people.

Ms. Perez: That seems a little bit extreme. I think it's better to give the facts about our products.

Mr. Yuan: I hate to disagree with you, but people don't remember facts—they remember images.

Ms. Perez: You may be right in part, but there's so much shock advertising these days. We need to try something unique—like using humor to give information.

Mr. Yuan: You may have something there. What would you suggest?

B Fill in the chart with these expressions. Then add the expressions in blue from the conversations on page 43.

I see your point, but . . .	I completely agree.	You're absolutely right!
Exactly!	No way!	I know what you mean, but . . .
Definitely!	I'm not sure I agree with you.	Yeah, but . . . I don't think so.

Agreeing with an opinion	Disagreeing with an opinion

C Pair work. **Answer the questions.**

1. Which expressions would you use when talking to a friend or coworker?
2. Which expressions would you be more likely to use with someone you didn't know as well?
3. What are some things that you disagree with your friends/family/coworkers about?
   Do you ever try to change their opinions?

D Pair work. **Choose role A or B, and think about reasons for your opinions.**
Then role-play these situations with your partner.

1. A: After finishing high school, you want to start your own business instead of going to university.
   B: You're A's friend. You think this is a terrible idea.

2. A: You want to set up a recycling program in your office.
   B: You're A's boss. You think this would be impractical.

3. A: You belong to Stop Hunger Now. You want to have a benefit concert to raise money.
   B: You're also a member. You think it's better just to ask people to donate money.

4. A: You're planning a class party. You want to have it in a restaurant so that people can get to know each other.
   B: You're A's classmate. You think a party at a dance club would be more fun.

Make an Impact

Lesson B | Take a stand.

1 GET READY TO READ

Take action!

WARM UP — What ads have made an impression on you? Why?

A Pair work. **Read each ad and discuss the questions below.**

No GMOs! Keep our food from being genetically modified!

Speak out against GMOs! Sunday, noon - 4:00

Don't be a part of the problem.

One Less Car.

Be part of the solution!

Eat Right!

Help us raise awareness about eating right.

Recycle Paper! Save Trees!

Make deforestation a thing of the past!

  **Do your part!**

Home, Sweet Home...

Need we say more?

1. In each ad above, what are people being encouraged to do or not to do?
2. Which ads do you think work well? Why?
3. *Irony* is using words or images in such a way that they mean the opposite, for example, to a person wearing an ugly tie you say, "Nice tie!" The ad with the homeless man is using *irony* to make its point. How?
4. What do you think "deforestation" means? Notice the root "forest" and the prefix "de-" which means "to take away."

World Link

Experts say that the biggest single step to curbing global warming is raising vehicular gas mileage standards. By requiring SUVs and other light trucks to get the same gas mileage as cars, 240 million tons of carbon dioxide per year would be saved by the end of the next decade.

▶ Ask & *Answer*

Have you ever seen an ad, poster, bumper sticker, or button like the ones above? What did it say? What was it encouraging people to do or not to do?

Reminder: Inferencing

Information is not always stated directly. Often a reader must infer, or make guesses about something, using information that is available in the reading.

A Pair work. The reading on page 47 is about a company that promotes the events below. What kind of company do you think it is? What do you think they want to have happen for each of these events? Discuss your ideas with your partner.

Buy Nothing Day   No Car Day   TV Turnoff Week

B Read the article on page 47. Then read the statements in the chart. Were these ideas stated in the article, or did you have to infer this information? Check the correct box. Then compare your answers with a partner.

	stated	inferred
1. Kalle Lasn made documentaries for public television in Canada for years.		
2. Kalle Lasn and his partners believe that advertising should be used to inform people, not just sell them products.		
3. The Culture Jammers Network is made up of people who are interested in social change.		
4. Lasn believes that people shouldn't just complain. They need to try to change things they're unhappy about.		
5. It's now possible to see some of Adbusters ads on cable TV stations.		

C Read the article again. Pay attention to details about ways Kalle Lasn thinks outside the box. Then complete the sentences below with information from the reading.

1. Unlike other advertisements, many of Adbuster's ads use _____ and _____ to promote a _____ message.

2. Culture Jammers hosts events such as _____, _____, and _____. The goal with these events is to _____.

3. To challenge how people think, some Culture Jammers hack into web sites in order to

   _____.

4. Lasn's motto is _____.

Real English
think outside the box = to think differently or in an original and creative way

D Pair work. Discuss the questions below.

1. What is the main point of the ad for "Hope" cigarettes?
2. If the mother of the baby in the fast-food ad could speak to the president of the company, what do you think she would say?

▶ **Ask & Answer**
Adbusters sponsors events like TV Turnoff Week. Think about your daily routine. What's one change you could make that would make a difference?

ADBUSTERS

THINK OUTSIDE THE BOX

Kalle Lasn was in a supermarket parking lot one afternoon when he had an experience that changed his life. In order to shop at the store, he needed to put money into the shopping cart to use it. Annoyed that he had to "pay to shop," Lasn jammed the coin into the cart so that it wouldn't work. It was an act of rebellion—the first of many—for Lasn.

Born in Estonia, Kalle Lasn moved to Australia as a young man and then later to Japan, where he founded a marketing research firm in Tokyo. Eventually, Lasn emigrated to Canada and for several years produced documentaries for public television. In the late 1980s, Lasn made an advertisement that spoke out against the logging industry and the deforestation going on in the Pacific Northwest. When he tried to show his ad on TV, though, no station in the region would give him airtime. In response, Lasn and a colleague founded Adbusters Media Foundation, a company dedicated to the "human right to communicate."

HARE TODAY.

GONE TOMORROW!

Be a considerate consumer. Don't buy fur.

Adbusters produces magazine, newspaper, and TV ads with a social message. Many use humor and irony to make their points: in one, for example, a man chain smokes a brand of cigarettes called "Hope." In another, a child is dressed in an outfit used in fast-food ads. Next to the child is a note from its mother telling the restaurant to leave her child alone.

Adbusters also has a magazine and a web site, The Culture Jammers Network, whose members include students, artists, and activists as well as educators and businesspeople interested in social change. Many of these "culture jammers" are working to raise awareness about different social issues by hosting events like "Buy Nothing Day," "No Car Day," and "TV Turnoff Week." Lasn and his partners hope these events will encourage people to think about questions such as:

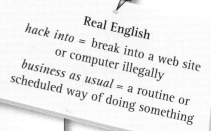

Real English
hack into = break into a web site or computer illegally
business as usual = a routine or scheduled way of doing something

- What kinds of things are we being encouraged to buy by the media?

- Should cars be our primary means of transportation?

- How are television and radio being used now? How *could* we be using them?

Some culture jammers are using other methods to challenge how people think. Some pretend to be shoppers. They move items in stores from one shelf to another making it difficult for people to find things easily. Other culture jammers hack into large corporate web sites and jam them so that they become unusable. The goal in both cases is to prevent "business as usual" and to get people to ask themselves questions such as "Why am I shopping here?" or "Why should I buy this product?"

Lasn and members of The Culture Jammers Network want to make people aware of social issues, but they also believe it's important to think of solutions, too. "[A lot of people] tell you everything that's wrong . . . but they never say much about how to fix these problems," says Lasn. [But] "there is plenty we can do. If you start despairing, you have lost everything."

Though many TV stations still won't show Adbusters' "uncommercials," some cable TV stations have started to. People all over the world have also joined the Culture Jammers Network and are doing their part to promote social change. Behind it all is Lasn's motto, "We can and must change the world."

A Read this letter to the editor of a newspaper.

NO CAR DAY

Find new ways to get there!

TV TURNOFF WEEK

Quit watching, start living!

Buy Nothing Day

Stop shopping and save the planet!

April 12

Dear Editor:

Your article about Kalle Lasn and Adbusters had some interesting ideas, especially about transportation. <u>No Car Day is a great idea for our city.</u> For one thing, a lot of drivers will learn how fast and modern our subway is. They might be more willing to use public transportation in the future. Also, people will get healthy exercise if they walk or bike. I started biking to work last year, and

it has made a huge difference in my energy level. And finally, a day without cars shows how much pollution they pour into the air. Wouldn't it be great to breathe clean air, even for just one day? I think we would be shocked by the difference. No Car Day is an idea whose time has come, and I hope the city council will support it.

Sincerely,
Natalia Moreno

B Reread the underlined sentence where Natalia gives her opinion.
This is the *topic sentence*. Then write the three ideas she includes to support her opinion.

1. _____
2. _____
3. _____

C Complete this topic sentence for your own letter to the editor. Then list three reasons for your opinion.

In my opinion, (TV Turnoff Week / Buy Nothing Day) is a (great / terrible) idea.

Reasons:
1. _____
2. _____
3. _____

D Write your own letter to the editor.

E Pair work. Exchange letters with a partner. Make two suggestions to help your partner improve his or her letter. If you don't like your partner's suggestions, disagree politely.

I think you need to explain your reasons a little more.

I see your point, but letters to the editor have to be short.

4 COMMUNICATION

Activity 1: What's your motto?

A Kalle Lasn's motto is "We can and must change the world." What's your personal motto? Choose one from the ones here or write your own.

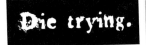

Through it all, keep smiling.

Be prepared.

Everyone deserves a second chance.

Accept what you can't change and change what you can't accept.

To thine own self be true.

Your idea: _____

Waste not, want not.

B Group work. Get into a group of three or four people. Tell your group what your motto is. Describe a situation in which your motto has helped you.

Activity 2: A public service announcement

A Pair work. **Listen to the Public Service Announcement. Then discuss the questions with a partner.** (CD Tracks 13 & 14)

1. What issue is the PSA trying to raise awareness about?
2. What is it telling people they should or shouldn't do?

> **Real English**
> *Public Service Announcements (PSAs) are short radio or TV ads used to raise public awareness about an issue.*

B Group work. **Work in groups of three to write a short PSA to raise awareness about a specific issue. Choose an issue from below or think of your own.**

- eating right
- driving safely
- recycling
- saving money
- promoting peace
- other: _____

C Class work. **Present your PSA to the class. As you listen to your classmates' PSAs, answer questions 1 and 2 in A for each.**

 Check out the CNN® video. **Practice your English online at elt.heinle.com/worldpass**

Unit 4: Make an Impact

A Match each word in blue with its meaning.

1. Animal rights activists have been campaigning for all of us to stop eating meat. ___
2. Surfing and scuba diving are two of my favorite vacation activities. ___
3. There has been an increase in activism among students in recent years. ___
4. My grandmother stays active with gardening, playing cards, and going to her senior citizens' club. ___
5. People should be proactive and prepare for natural disasters. ___
6. Ms. Jemison will be the acting manager until we hire someone permanently. ___

a. working for social change (noun)
b. things that people do for a purpose or for relaxation (noun)
c. busy doing things (adjective)
d. taking charge of things before they happen (adjective)
e. temporary (adjective)
f. people who work for social change (noun)

B Complete the sentences with a form of a word from A. Add an article (a, an, the) where necessary.

1. When I was younger, I led a very _____ life. I played on two sports teams, and I went hiking in the mountains almost every weekend.
2. Skydiving is _____ that I've never tried. It's just too dangerous.
3. It's better to take a _____ approach to pollution than to spend money on it later.
4. My best friend is _____ for an environmental group called "Save the Oceans."
5. The new _____ principal of the school held a meeting to introduce herself to the teachers.
6. "Adbusters" is an example of _____ against overconsumption.

> ### I didn't know that!
> *Candidate* comes from the Latin word *candidus*, which means "bright, shining white." In ancient Rome, candidates who hoped to be elected to government office would wear bright white clothes. The English word *candid*, which means "honest," comes from the same source. But how many *candidates* are really *candid*?

C Fill in the blanks with the related strong adjective in the box.

> boiling   gorgeous   terrifying   enormous   freezing   tiny   horrendous

1. The weather was <u>cold</u> yesterday, and it's even colder today. In fact, it's _____.
2. My dog is <u>small</u>, but my sister's dog is absolutely _____.
3. Our classroom is usually too <u>warm</u>, but today it's _____ in here.
4. That movie isn't just <u>scary</u>. I think it's _____!
5. Her old house was <u>big</u>, but her new house is really _____.
6. The storm wasn't just <u>bad</u>. It was truly _____.
7. Carmen isn't just <u>beautiful</u>. I think she's absolutely _____.

D Rewrite the sentences using one of the phrases from the box.

Word combinations with *action*	
no further action is needed	swing into action
plan of action	call for action
take action	put your ideas into action

1. The city government must <u>do something</u> to solve the transportation crisis.
_____

2. Firefighters are always ready to <u>start working immediately</u> in case of any emergency.
_____

3. We have received your application, and at this time, <u>you don't need to do anything else</u>.
_____

4. You have a great plan, and now it's time to <u>start doing something about your idea</u>.
_____

5. "Save the Earth" has issued a <u>request for help</u> to stop the construction of a giant hotel on Paradise Beach.
_____

6. We need to develop a <u>list of future activities</u> for our campaign to improve education in this country.
_____

E Review these words from the reading "Think Outside the Box" on page 47. Circle their meanings.

1. rebellion (para 1)   a. getting ready   b. making noise   c. fighting back
2. logging (para 2)   a. cutting trees   b. building houses   c. killing animals
3. primary (para 4)   a. most expensive   b. most important   c. most unusual
4. despairing (para 6)   a. giving up   b. making plans   c. being hopeful
5. promote (para 7)   a. stop   b. protest   c. increase

In Other Words

If you are apathetic, you are not willing to make an effort to change things: *My parents are completely apathetic about environmental problems.*

If you are indifferent to something, you have no feelings about it: *Alan was crazy about Cathy, but she was indifferent to him.*

Uninterested means not interested: *I'm completely uninterested in baseball. I think it's boring.*

Disinterested is NOT the same as uninterested. It means "not influenced by personal reasons": *We need a disinterested person to decide what is fair.*

An obligation is a legal or moral requirement: *Teachers have an obligation to treat all their students fairly.*

A responsibility means the state of being in charge of something: *Janet will have responsibility for the new advertising campaign.*

Duties (usually plural) are parts of a job: *My duties include feeding and taking care of the zoo animals.*

A requirement is something that is essential or needed: *The requirements for that job are a master's degree and five years' experience.*

Watch out!

negative prefixes
The prefixes *a-, un-, in-/il-/im-* used with adjectives all have the meaning "not" or "without." However, you have to learn which prefix goes with which adjective.

perfect	→	*imperfect*	~~unperfect, aperfect~~
political	→	*apolitical*	~~unpolitical, impolitical~~
motivated	→	*unmotivated*	~~amotivated, immotivated~~

1 VOCABULARY FOCUS

A mysterious disappearance

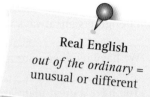

Real English

out of the ordinary =
unusual or different

 You are going to read a news article based on a police report.
What kinds of news events are typically in a police report?

A Read the article. What kind of police report is it based on? Check (✓) the box.

☐ burglary report ☐ traffic report ☐ missing persons report

Daily Times Tuesday, September 22

Somerville Man Sought

A Somerville man, is being **sought** by police after he disappeared on Friday afternoon. Adam Martin, a well-known family man and **devoted** father of two, left home September 19th and never returned.

Police say that Martin, 39, went out at 2:00 P.M. with his tool kit, saying he was answering a **distress call** from his friend Devin, who was **stranded** on the Highway 92 with a flat tire. By late Friday evening, his wife Susan was very worried. She considered calling the police, but decided to wait until the following morning to contact **authorities**.

Martin, a banker, had the day off, because his branch of First Bank Savings & Loan was closed for renovations. "He seemed very relaxed and happy to have some time away from the office," said his wife. "I didn't notice anything out of the ordinary."

Police are eager to question Martin about a bank transfer he made late Thursday night. "A large amount of cash was transferred from our branch in Somerville to the main branch in Boston late Thursday night," said First Bank

manager Frank de Leo. "The money was then withdrawn in Boston on Friday afternoon."

Police are speaking with a **witness** who may have seen Martin on Friday afternoon in a bright blue truck with an unidentified young female passenger. The female is also being sought for questioning regarding her **involvement** in the case.

Mrs. Martin is keeping her hopes up. "Adam has **seemingly vanished**—which is completely unlike him," says Susan. "But I know that this story will have a positive **outcome**. I know that he will return soon."

A blue truck was found on Monday about a half mile from the airport. It has been **identified** as Mr. Martin's. Inside the truck were some bank **documents** and a pair of sunglasses. Police are studying this **evidence** carefully.

Police may have a **theory** about what happened, but are not talking at the moment. They urge anyone with information regarding this **incident** to call the Somerville Police at 800-555-TIPS.

B Write the words in A next to their definitions below.

1. a person who sees an event: __witness__
2. official papers: _____
3. looked for: _____
4. apparently: _____
5. an emergency call for help: _____
6. recognized: _____
7. officials, in this case the police: _____
8. disappeared suddenly: _____

9. words or objects that prove something is true: _____
10. in a helpless situation and unable to move: _____
11. event: _____
12. result: _____
13. dedicated: _____
14. participation: _____
15. an explanation not yet proven to be true: _____

C Pair work. What do you think happened to Adam Martin? Discuss with a partner.

▶▶ Vocabulary Builder ▲

Some nouns are usually found in the plural. Read an update on the situation. Use the plural nouns in the box to complete the information.

> authorities   premises   outskirts   whereabouts

(1) _____ are still searching for a missing Somerville man who disappeared last Friday. Although they don't know Adam Martin's exact (2) _____, they think he may now be in California. Yesterday they inspected a room at the Golden Gable Hotel, located on the (3) _____ of Boston. It is believed Martin stayed there on the night of Friday, September 19. When police searched the (4) _____, they found a receipt for two airline tickets to Los Angeles.

2 LISTENING

A chance meeting

Think about a time you ran into someone. Who was it? Where were you? How did you feel?

A Pair work. Look at this photo. What do you think the situation is? Discuss your ideas with a partner.

B Listen. What is the relationship between Claudia and Cara? Check (✓) the box. (CD Tracks 15 & 16)

- ☐ They are former classmates being reunited.
- ☐ They are sisters who were adopted at birth by different parents.
- ☐ They are college friends who survived a train crash five years ago.

> **Real English**
> *run into* = to see someone by chance
> *adopt* = to legally make someone else's child part of your family

C Listen to Claudia and Cara talk about their lives. Read each item. If it's the same for the girls, write "S." If it's different, write "D." (CD Track 17)

1. _D_ religious background
2. ___ where they grew up
3. ___ their physical appearance
4. ___ college
5. ___ where they live now
6. ___ relationship with Josh now
7. ___ favorite food

> **Real English**
> We use *to say the least* to express that a statement is even more surprising or serious than has been suggested. *My father was angry, to say the least.*

D The phrases below are used in the interview. Listen and circle to complete each answer. (CD Track 18)

1. An only child has no / many brothers and sisters.
2. When you can't tell two people apart, it's because they look the same / different.
3. A twist of fate is an expected / unexpected event.
4. If two people have a lot in common they have similar / different characteristics and habits.

E Pair work. Compare your answers in C with a partner. Then, use the phrases in D and your own words to retell Claudia's and Cara's story.

> ▶ **Ask & Answer**
> Is adoption common in your country? Why or why not?

A Read about the disappearance of Jim Thompson.

Jim Thompson was a young American when he arrived in Thailand in 1945, two days after the end of World War II. For the next 22 years, he lived in Thailand, working to revitalize the Thai silk industry, which had all but disappeared. As the founder of his own silk company, he also promoted Thai arts and crafts. Today you can tour the Jim Thompson House in Bangkok, one of the finest examples of traditional Thai architecture in the city.

In March of 1967, while vacationing in Malaysia's Cameron Highlands, Jim Thompson went for a walk. He never returned. There was no distress call, and no witnesses ever came forward with information about his disappearance or his whereabouts. The question is: What happened to Jim Thompson?

B Pair work. Look back at the modal phrases in blue below. Which theories about Jim Thompson are more certain? Underline them. Which are less certain? Circle them. Then compare your ideas with a partner.

There are many theories surrounding Jim Thompson's disappearance:

1. During the war Jim Thompson was trained by the OSS, which later became the CIA (Central Intelligency Agency) in the United States. <u>He may have worked for the CIA after the war ended.</u> If that is true, he might have been killed because of his connection to the CIA.

2. Some people say that he could have decided to start a new life somewhere else, so he disappeared on purpose. Others point to the fact that he left his cigarettes and lighter behind when he went on the walk. He must have planned to return, they say.

3. It's been well over 35 years since he disappeared. Most people agree that he couldn't have survived.

C Read more statements about Jim Thompson. Choose the appropriate response for each.

1. Jim Thompson lived in Thailand for 22 years.
   a. He may have loved the country and its people.
   b. He must have loved the country and its people.

2. Six months after Jim's disappearance, his sister was murdered by a burglar in Chicago.
   a. That's surprising. There may have been a connection.
   b. That's surprising. There must not have been any connection.

3. He could have fallen into a cave and died.
   a. I agree. I'm sure that happened.
   b. Anything is possible, I guess.

4. I don't know anything about Jim Thompson.
   a. You must not have read the book about him.
   b. You must have read the book about him.

5. He couldn't have disappeared on purpose.
   a. We can conclude that he didn't disappear on purpose.
   b. We can't conclude that he disappeared on purpose.

D Pair work. Read the conversations about Jim Thompson. Rewrite the underlined sentences using modals of speculation. Compare your answers with a partner. Then discuss what you think happened to him.

1. A: <u>Maybe he was kidnapped</u>.

   _____

   B: <u>It's certain that didn't happen</u>. There was no ransom note.

   _____

   A: <u>It's likely he had a heart attack</u>.

   _____

   B: <u>That's possible</u>.

   _____

2. A: <u>We can conclude he died in the jungle</u>.

   _____

   B: <u>It's possible he didn't die there</u>. After all, none of his clothing or bones were ever found or identified.

   _____

E Pair work. Read the situations below. Discuss them with a partner.

1. You went into your office last Sunday to pick up some documents. You surprised your coworker, who was at his desk. He seemed nervous. What do you think he was doing?

2. You arrived home late one night and saw someone climbing into your neighbor's kitchen window. Who do you think it was?

3. You were on a date when your dinner partner's cell phone rang. He/She looked upset and left the table to take the call. Who do you think was on the other end of the phone line?

F Group work. Join another pair and exchange ideas. Then vote on the most probable explanation for each situation.

The expression "raining cats and dogs" is used to mean "raining heavily." However, fish, frogs, snakes, and even apples have actually fallen from the sky! Where do these "strange rains" come from? Scientists think strong winds pick up the items and carry them a short distance before dropping them on the heads of very surprised onlookers.

4 SPEAKING
The boss's birthday cake

A Read the situation below. Then look at the expressions in blue and match the sentence parts.

The office workers at Zigert Co. planned to have a birthday party for their boss at lunch time today. Yesterday at 5 P.M., they put Mr. Ramero's birthday cake in the office refrigerator. When they opened the fridge this morning at 8 A.M., it was empty. What happened?

> **Making speculations**
>
> Less certain
> 1. I wonder if the cleaners __g__
> 2. I suppose a thief ____
> 3. I suspect that our boss ____
> 4. I'm pretty sure that Jason ____
> 5. I'm convinced/certain/positive that Mary ____
> 6. It's impossible that we ____
> 7. There's no doubt that the cake ____
> More certain

a. stole the cake. He loves desserts.
b. took it home with him yesterday. It had his name on it.
c. forgot to order it. We know that Carol picked it up.
d. could have broken into the office last night.
e. ate it. She was in the office until 10:00 last night.
f. was gone when we got to work.
g. ~~emptied out the fridge.~~

B List five possible explanations for each of these situations.

Your class started fifteen minutes ago.
Your teacher still isn't there.

1. _stuck in a traffic jam_
2. _____
3. _____
4. _____
5. _____

You are at the train station to meet your friend after work. Your friend has never been there before. You have been waiting for an hour.

1. _gotten lost_
2. _____
3. _____
4. _____
5. _____

C Pair work. Talk about the situations in B, and respond to your partner's explanations.

> *I wonder if Mr. Frikson is stuck in a traffic jam.*

> *No way! He walks to school.*

> **Responding to speculation**
>
> Definitely!
> You're probably right.
> You may be right.
> Well, maybe, but . . .
> That hardly seems likely.
> No way! *(informal)*

D Pair work. Think of a mysterious situation and write it down. Give it to another pair.

> *You come to class late. When you open the door, no one is there, but there's a big empty box on the teacher's desk.*

E Pair work. Role-play explaining the situation you received.

> *Somebody must have . . .*

Unexplained phenomena

WARM UP Have you ever witnessed an unexplained phenomenon or strange event? What happened?

A Read the two letters written to a science magazine.

B Now read the letters again along with the responses. Pay attention to the words in blue.

C Match each word in blue with its definition.

1. happening often or regularly: _____
2. prior, happening before: _____
3. break down, stop working: _____
4. saw or noticed something: _____
5. to cause something to happen: _____
6. guessed: _____
7. mysterious, hard to explain: _____
8. knowing or sensing something even though you don't have all the facts: _____

D Pair work. For each situation, circle two facts and underline one theory. Then, compare your answers with a partner. Which words helped you to decide which were facts and which were theories?

▶**Ask & *Answer***

What do you think of the scientific explanations for each of the events in B? Do you think there could be other causes for each? What?

● Ask the expert ●

This week's topic:

Unexplained Phenomena

My husband Max has an unusual problem: he **routinely** causes light bulbs, TVs, and computers to blow up when he's nearby. Even the batteries in his watch only last a week or so, and then they stop working. Do you have any idea what might **trigger** these events? For some **inexplicable** reason, they usually happen when my husband is stressed or upset about something. Do you have any idea what's going on?

Signed,
In the Dark

Dear In the Dark,

Believe it or not, your husband's condition is not that uncommon. Although there's no definite evidence yet, some researchers have **speculated** that your husband's condition might be created by electronic impulses in the brain. This electricity somehow leaves the body and can cause electronic devices (like computers) to **malfunction.**

I saw a show on TV last night about an 11-year-old British girl who says she is able to recall her past life. The child said that in her **previous** life she was a nineteenth-century German farmer named Hans Treuter. The most amazing thing I **observed** was that when hypnotized, the child spoke fluent German (a language neither she nor her parents speak). My **intuition** tells me that this story isn't real, but I'd like to know what scientists have to say.

Signed,
Doubting Thomas

Dear Thomas,

You're right to question stories like these. Many scientists suspect that cases of past life recall may be due to an extraordinary memory. In other words, a person is able to remember in great detail something he or she has seen, heard, or read—even if this only happened very briefly, or when the person was very young.

A   Pair work. Read the three facts at the beginning of the reading. Then skim the remainder of the passage. What may have been the cause of the disappearances? Tell your partner.

Mystery World

Consider the facts below:

1. Over the last twenty years, hundreds of cargo ships—many as big as a soccer field—have mysteriously disappeared or been destroyed in the North Atlantic and near the tip of South America and South Africa.

2. The Bermuda Triangle, roughly the area between southern Florida, Puerto Rico, and Bermuda, has been the site of many ship and aircraft disappearances over the last hundred years.

5   3. In the Pacific Ocean, just off the coast of central Japan, there is a region known as "The Devil's Sea"—given its name in 1955 after ten ships vanished. The area has been named a danger zone by the Japanese government for the number of ships that are routinely, and inexplicably, lost there.

For years, scientists struggled to explain these events. Many speculated that bad weather or machine malfunction were responsible. But now there is evidence that may shed new light on the disappearances. Satellites
10   set up by the European Space Agency have recently identified enormous waves far out in the oceans. These "rogue waves" are often nearly 30 meters high, or about the size of a twelve-story building. They often rise unexpectedly, like monstrous walls of water from the sea, crashing down with great force, and then, they disappear.

Though waves this size have been part of nautical* folklore for centuries, scientists believed that they were extremely rare (occurring only once every 10,000 years). The satellite data, though, proves that they are more
15   common than once thought. Scientists now also suspect that these waves may have been responsible for many of the unexplained disappearances of low-flying aircraft and ships over the years.

So, how and why do waves like these form? Until very recently, oceanographers** thought that rogues were the result of many smaller waves joining together to form a giant wave. But in analyzing the recent satellite images collected by the European Space Agency, scientists have noted that rogues appear to form most often in places
20   where waves of different strengths come together from different directions. At the southernmost tip of Africa, for example, where the Atlantic and Indian Oceans meet, it is quite common for waves to crash into each other. Combined with the strong ocean currents in the region, waves may then grow to enormous height. This theory may explain the occurrence of rogue waves in similar locations around the globe (such as at the tip of South America) known for colliding waves and strong ocean currents. However, it does not explain why the waves form in places
25   where there are no fast-moving ocean currents—such as in the North Sea.

To understand why rogue waves might form in places like the North Sea and other spots around the globe, oceanographers have turned to studying the weather and its effect on the ocean. Some scientists now believe that fast-moving winds blowing for long periods of time over waves in the open ocean might create a rogue monster. However, this has been observed most often in the southern oceans, and still does not fully explain why huge waves
30   form in places like the North Sea. Still, scientists are hoping that by studying weather patterns they may be able to predict where rogue waves are likely to develop.

Though scientists are beginning to understand more about rogue waves, there is still a lot to learn. However, now that it is clear that these waves are more common than once thought, efforts are being made to improve ships' safety and to minimize the loss of life.

35   *nautical: related to sailing and the sea   **oceanographers: scientists who study the oceans

B Complete the sentences below with the appropriate words or phrases from the article.

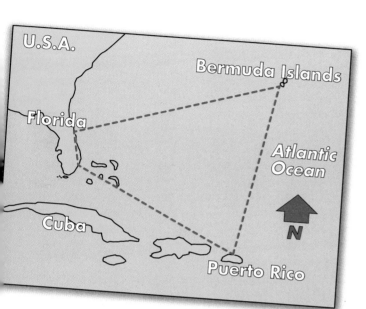

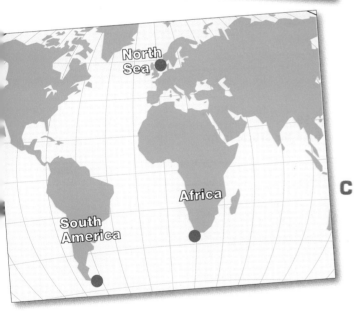

_____ 1. Ships and aircraft have _____ in areas such as the _____ , the Bermuda Triangle, and the _____ .

_____ 2. It's possible that bad weather or _____ were responsible for these disappearances.

_____ 3. Recently, _____ identified enormous waves far out in the oceans that are nearly _____ high.

_____ 4. Although scientists once believed that the waves happened only _____ years, it is now clear that they are more _____ than once thought.

_____ 5. Scientists now suspect that the _____ may have been caused by these waves.

_____ 6. Rogue waves seem to happen in places, such as _____ and _____ where waves of different _____ come together from _____.

_____ 7. It's also possible that these enormous waves are also caused by _____.

_____ 8. Even though there is a lot that scientists still don't understand about rogue waves, shipping companies are now trying to _____.

C Read the statements in B and decide if each is a fact or a theory. Write the correct letter (*F* or *T*) next to each statement above.

> **Distinguishing fact from theory**
>
> A fact is something that can be checked and proven. A theory is a possible explanation for something. When discussing a theory, speculative words and phrases are often used such as:
>
> *may*   *might*   *could*
> *It seems/appears . . .*   *It's possible . . .*
> *We suspect . . .*   *We think/believe . . .*

▶ **Ask & *Answer***

Name another "unexplained phenomenon" (e.g., ghosts, UFOs) that you know of. How could it be explained?

D Pair work. **Close your book. Summarize the article with a partner. Include something you learned from the reading that surprised you.**

Writing a summary

A Read the article below.

FIRST AT THE ROOF OF THE WORLD *by Michelle Gao*

Tibet is one of the coldest inhabited places on Earth, with winter temperatures plunging as low as -40 degrees Celsius. Until very recently, scientists believed that the first inhabitants of Tibet arrived only around 4,000 years ago, after the end of its most recent Ice Age. They theorized that previously the Tibetan plateau had been covered by ice a mile thick.

Then, in 1986, a researcher from Hong Kong University named David Zhang made a remarkable discovery. High on a mountain slope, about 85 km from the city of Lhasa, he found 19 human handprints and footprints, embedded in ancient rock at the edge of a hot spring. But the real surprise didn't come until 1999. That's when he and his colleagues tried a technique called optical dating, which revealed that the prints were actually more than 20,000 years old.

Zhang determined that the handprints and footprints were made by six different people, two of them children. He also found the remains of a stove there. It seems likely that this group of early Tibetans came to the hot spring to take refuge from the extreme cold of the Ice Age. Zhang says "The findings mean that human settlement occured here 16,000 years earlier than scientists had thought, and also that human beings had the ability to adapt to such a cold environment."

But why did they press their hands and feet into the mud? Zhang thinks they did it out of curiosity, or maybe just for fun. The soft mud around the spring preserved the prints when it later turned into a form of stone called travertine. In the future, Zhang hopes to explore further on the Tibetan Plateau to collect more evidence of early Tibetan settlements.

B Review the expressions used to distinguish fact from theory on page 59.
Then complete the chart with brief notes about theories and facts from the article in A.

Facts	Theories

C Complete a summary of the article in A. Include at least three facts and three theories.

An article entitled "First at the Roof of the World," by Michelle Gao, discusses . . .

Writing a summary

A summary is a written condensation of the most important points in a text in your own words. You can rearrange or reorganize the ideas to make them clearer. As a general rule, you should not copy more than five words in a row from the text.

D Pair work. Exchange summaries with your partner and locate the facts and theories. Are all the most important points included?

Activity 1: The sixth sense

A The "sixth sense" is often defined as a strong hunch (feeling) that a person has about something or someone. Read about one mother's experience.

I HAD A HUNCH . . .

Kathy Sansano arrived home from work two months ago at 7:00 in the evening. "Normally, my husband is home before me, but when I got in, his briefcase was there, but he wasn't," recalls Sansano. She just assumed that he went to the store for something. Sansano began preparing dinner, but couldn't shake the feeling that something was wrong. "I just started feeling very anxious and had to sit down. Five minutes later my husband phoned to say that our son had been injured in a football game at school."

Luckily, the boy only suffered a broken wrist, but Sansano still can't explain how she knew something was wrong. "It might have been 'mother's intuition,'" she laughs. "My son and I have always been very close."

Science identifies five basic senses that humans use to experience the world. There is now evidence that humans may also possess a sixth sense—or an intuition about people or events. Recent studies done suggest that insects and animals release odorless chemicals called pheromones into the environment to signal emotions such as fear or aggression. When another creature of the same species senses the chemical (via its nose), a certain behavior is triggered in that creature; for example, it will prepare to fight or to protect itself.

Scientists believe that humans long ago may have communicated using these kinds of chemical signals, and that we continue to produce and sense pheromones, although less than our ancestors did. It has been described this way: "How often do we hear someone say, for example, 'I walked into the room, and something just didn't seem right.'" It may be that the person is sensing chemical messages that have been produced by others—even if those individuals are no longer present. Kathy Sansano's husband may have left the house feeling afraid and worried about their son. When Kathy got home, she sensed his anxiety—which may explain the unease she then experienced.

B Pair work. Was Kathy Sansano's hunch just a coincidence or does the article suggest another possibility? Discuss your ideas with a partner.

Activity 2: Have any of these things ever happened to you?

A Look at the list below. Choose one, or think of something else that happened to you that you couldn't explain.

- I had a feeling that something was going to happen, and then it did.
- I had a dream that something was going to happen, and it came true.
- I started thinking about a person, and then he or she called or came to visit me.

B Group work. Get into a group of four people. Tell your group the story of what happened to you. Your group listens and asks you questions. Then, each person in your group offers a possible explanation for the event.

 **Check out the CNN® video.**   **Practice your English online at** elt.heinle.com/worldpass

A Study the word combinations in the box. Write the letter of the word combination with a meaning similar to that of the underlined phrase after each sentence below.

> **Word combinations with *mystery***
>
> a. It's a mystery to me.   d. a murder mystery
> b. solve/unravel a mystery   e. the mystery deepens.
> c. give someone an air of mystery   f. a complete/total mystery

1. We still don't know what happened to Jim Thompson. Every year, <u>we understand it less</u>. ___
2. <u>I have absolutely no idea</u> how that bird got into my apartment! ___
3. I like to relax by reading <u>a detective novel about a killing</u>, but I can never figure out who committed the crime. ___
4. I don't know how birds find their way when they migrate. It's <u>something I can't understand</u>. ___
5. Her exotic clothes and unusual accent <u>made the woman seem unusual and interesting</u>. ___
6. It took three years of hard work by police detectives to <u>figure out what happened</u> in the case of the missing baby. ___

B Use your dictionary to help you add these nouns to the correct group.

> sleuth   clue   puzzle   speculation
> investigator   enigma   evidence   hypothesis

1. proof, information, _____, _____
2. detective, researcher, _____, _____
3. question, mystery, _____, _____
4. theory, guess, _____, _____

Incorrect: *My wife is having three cats.*   Correct: *My wife <u>has</u> three cats.*

Expansion Pages

C Find the best noun for each verb.

1. We solve ___.   a. a solution
2. We answer ___.   b. a question
3. We find ___.   c. a fact
4. We catch ___.   d. a mystery
5. We state ___.   e. a criminal

D The prefix *mal–* means "bad." Complete the sentences with a word from the box. Check the meaning in your dictionary if necessary.

> malfunction   malnourished   malpractice
> maltreat   malcontent   malformed

1. Cheryl is a real _____. She's always unhappy with everything at the office, but she complains every time they try to change something!
2. The doctor lost his job because of _____ . He made some very serious mistakes with medication, and almost killed two patients.
3. The plane crash was caused by a _____ in the plane's electronic system.
4. The newspaper had sad photos of skinny, _____ children who were suffering from the famine.
5. My little brother was born with a _____ foot, but the surgery was successful and now he can walk without problems.
6. The dog's previous owner used to _____ him, so now he's afraid of people.

In Other Words

A **theory** is a possible explanation for something that has reasons behind it: *Scientists have a theory that the dinosaurs disappeared because of climate change.*

A **guess** is an attempt to say what is true or what will happen without knowing exactly: *My guess is that many people will be absent from class tomorrow.*

If you have a **hunch** about something, you have a feeling or intuition about it: *I have a hunch you'll find your missing wallet at home.*

If you **search** for something, you look for it very systematically and carefully: *An airplane searched for any sign of the missing boat.*

Look for is a more general term: *I'm looking for Anne / my keys / a better job.*

Hunt for is informal and means look around in a large area: *The kids hunted for shells on the beach.*

Watch out! adopt and adapt
Don't confuse these two very similar verbs. *Adopt* means to take legal responsibility for a child: *Mr. and Mrs. Lee adopted a little girl.* *Adapt* means to change something to make it suitable: *The movie was adapted for a TV series.*

1 VOCABULARY FOCUS

7/7

Trends in the workplace

WARM UP One trend in the workplace is that more people are telecommuting than before. Another trend is that people are working with flexible schedules. Can you think of other trends?

A **Read what these people are saying about trends or issues in business today. Match each person to the item they are talking about.**

☐ fair treatment of women ☐ downsizing (reducing staff) ☐ mail-order businesses

1. Jerome

I got my first job two years ago and then there was a downturn in the economy. Just my luck! First, my employer cut back on production. Then, when there wasn't enough work to go around, they started laying off people. About half of my coworkers had to find new jobs! My friends tell me I should look for a new job. Others tell me I should stick with this company for a while longer. I can't figure out what to do!

2. Linda

Let's face it—in the workplace, women still don't have the same opportunities as men. I've worked for the same company for ten years. I got passed over for a promotion last year. I found out the job went to a younger man with less experience. I handed in my notice last week and I feel good about quitting. I'm going back to school for an MBA. Will it help me get ahead in my next job? Who knows? One thing is certain: I'm not going to give up until I get what I want—equal treatment at work.

3. Kristin

In today's business climate, you've got to be clever—come up with ideas that others haven't thought of yet. Take my friend Anezka, an organic apple farmer. Five years ago, her business wasn't making a profit. It was about to go under. Then organic fruit really caught on. Suddenly it seemed that everyone wanted to buy her organic apples! She then decided to try something new: She set up a mail-order business so her customers could order her apples from home and get them quickly. Sales took off and Anezka made even more money. Now she's thinking about retiring early.

B Look at the expressions in A. Match them with their definitions. Which ones are used in a positive way? Which ones are used in a negative or neutral way?

1. cut back on _c_
2. lay off _h_
3. stick with _f_
4. figure out _j_
5. pass over _b_
6. find out _g_
7. hand in _l_
8. get ahead _m_
9. give up _e_
10. come up with _k_
11. go under _a_
12. catch on _i_
13. set up _n_
14. take off _d_

a. go bankrupt
b. not notice; ignore
c. decrease
d. increase dramatically
e. stop trying
f. continue
g. discover
h. stop employing someone
i. become popular
j. understand or solve
k. think of
l. give to someone
m. be successful
n. organize and start

2 LISTENING

Pretending to work

Do you ever goof off at school or work?
What do you usually do to avoid working or studying?

A David and Marc are being interviewed about a book that was recently published in France. Listen and complete the information about the book. (CD Tracks 19 & 20)

Author: _Corinne Maier_
Name of the book in English: _____
What the book is about: _____
_____

What kind of book is it: ☐ self-help ☐ historical fiction ☐ satire

Real English
goof off = to waste time and avoid working

B Which statements would David agree with?
Which ones would Marc agree with? Circle your answers.

David
1. We go to work because it's necessary.   Yes   No
2. Most readers can't understand the book.   Yes   No
3. The book was very funny.   Yes   No

Marc
1. The book had a positive tone.   Yes   No
2. The book encourages people not to try hard at work.   Yes   No

>> **Vocabulary Builder** ▲

A. Read the sentences below. What do you think each underlined phrase means?

1. We didn't budget enough money and had to get by on only $20 a day. _Survive, live on_
2. Roberto was sick and got behind at work. _fall back, become_
3. You need an employee ID to get into the building. _enter_ _be with work_
4. We were so busy we couldn't get away from the office until midnight. _leave, escape_
5. I'm busy now. Can I get back to you later today? _call back, respond, reply_

B. Now complete the sentences below using the correct form of the underlined phrases above.

1. Let's drive out Third Avenue so that we can _get away_ from all this traffic.
2. If we wait to buy tickets until later, we may not be able to _get into_ the theater.
3. The airline lost my suitcase and I had to _get by_ with just the clothes I had.
4. The travel agent promised to _get behind_ us later today with information about flights.
5. Bill _get behind_ on his credit card payments, and now he owes the bank over $5,000.

Pair work. **Listen again. What tips does the author give? Complete each one below. Would you do each one? Why or why not? Explain to a partner.** (CD Track 21)

1. _Pretend_ to be a smoker.
2. Hide a _____ inside a work _____.
3. Be nice to _____ workers.
4. Never accept a position of _____.
5. Go for the most _____ position.
6. _____.
7. _____.

> ▶ **Ask & Answer**
>
> What do you think of Corinne Maier's opinions about work? Do you agree or disagree with her ideas? Why?

D Pair work. **Add one or two tips to the list in C. Then share your ideas with another pair.**

> *You should pretend to be sick. That way you can take a lot of time off.*

3 LANGUAGE FOCUS
Phrasal verbs

A **These coworkers are talking about their company and its advertising plan. Read their statements. Underline six more phrasal verbs.**

> *In this economic climate, a lot of companies are <u>going under</u>. I'm worried that our company, too, will go bankrupt and will have to <u>lay off</u> some staff.*

> *I don't think we should make any drastic changes. Let's stick with our current strategy.*

> *We need to set up a marketing research team. The team should then come up with some new ideas for an ad campaign.*

> *Well, even though times are tough, we shouldn't cut back on our advertising budget.*

> *No, that sounds like we're giving up. I'm sure we can figure out a solution.*

> **Understanding phrasal verbs**
>
> A phrasal verb is a group of words, usually a verb + particle such as *give up*, used as a verb. The particle *(up)* looks like a preposition but functions as part of the verb. Note the difference in meaning below:
> *give* = offer something
> *give up* = quit or stop doing something

B **A transitive verb takes an object. An intransitive verb does not. Decide if each phrasal verb in A is transitive or intransitive. If it is transitive, circle the object. Then write the phrasal verbs in the correct column below.**

Transitive verb	Object	Intransitive verb
lay off	some staff	going under

C Rewrite the sentences below using the phrasal verbs in the box.

carry out	come up with	hand in	pass over	think about
~~catch on~~	get ahead	hang on	put off	

1. Do you think this style will <u>become popular</u> next season?   _Do you think this style will catch on next season?_
2. It's impossible to <u>succeed</u> in this competitive world.   _It's impossible to get ahead in this competitive world._
3. I <u>submitted</u> the final version of my proposal yesterday.   _hand in_
4. Are you <u>considering</u> hiring him?   _think about_
5. She was <u>not chosen</u> for the new position.   _pass over_
6. In my new job, I have to <u>perform</u> many challenging tasks.   _carry out_
7. We'll have to <u>postpone</u> the meeting until next week.   _put off_
8. Can you <u>think of</u> any new ideas?   _come up with_
9. If I can <u>wait</u> until the summer, I'll get a long break then.   _hang on_

D Group work. **Get into a group of three people and work together on this problem.**
Use the phrasal verbs in the box (and others of your own) to answer the questions.

carry out	come up with	set up	think about	catch on	figure out	take off

You work for an ice cream company that is about to go under. You desperately need to come up with a new flavor
to win back customers. Discuss these questions and use the phrasal verbs in the box for your discussion.

1. What is the name of the new flavor? _____
2. How will you sell it? _____
3. Where will you sell it? _____
4. Who are your target customers? _____
5. What is your advertising slogan? _____

To test the new flavor, we could set up a
booth in the mall and give away samples . . .

We need to come up with an effective
way to advertise the new flavor.

E Class activity. **Present your idea to the class. Vote on the best idea.**

World Link

While vanilla and chocolate are the most popular
flavors of ice cream, other more interesting flavors
are found around the world. Ice creams flavored
with fish, orchids, and chicken wings are offered in
Japan. And a restaurant in California even features
garlic-flavored ice cream! Yum . . . ?

4 SPEAKING

I can agree to that.

A Pair work. Janet and her boss are solving a problem at work.
Read the conversation and answer the questions that follow.
Compare your answers with a partner.

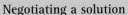

Negotiating a solution

Mr. Blair: Janet, I need you to present the sales report on Monday.

Janet: You do? But that's not possible. Today is Thursday, and I usually spend a week writing it!

Mr. Blair: I know. But I just found out that our new company president will be arriving from New York at 9:00. And you have to remember that this will be his first visit to our office. Would you consider working on Saturday if I give you the day off on Tuesday?

Janet: I'm afraid I can't. My sister's wedding is this Saturday.

Mr. Blair: Well, bear in mind that the sales meeting is the first thing on Monday morning now.

Janet: Hmm. I have an idea. If you'll let two other people work with me today, I could put the report together tomorrow.

Mr. Blair: OK, I can agree to that. Rick and Sandy can help you.

Janet: And maybe your assistant could make the photocopies?

Mr. Blair: That will be fine.

Janet: OK, then . . . I'd better get to work!

1. What does Mr. Blair want?   2. What does Janet want?   3. What agreement do they make?

B Complete the boxes with the expressions the speakers used for these things.

Bargaining	Bringing in facts
Would you consider . . . if I . . . ?	Bear in mind that . . .
_____	_____
Accepting	**Refusing**
_____	_____
_____	_____

C Pair work. Choose a role and plan what you will say. Then work with your partner to reach an agreement.

Role #1:
You are a coffee shop owner who
wants to keep costs down
- The price of coffee has gone up
- A new coffee shop in the neighborhood could put you out of business
- You are planning to expand the shop and need to cut down on costs

Role #2:
You are a coffee shop employee who
wants a raise (decide how much)
- You work 6 A.M.–2 P.M.–the busiest time
- You haven't had a raise in two years
- The new coffee shop pays its employees more
- You've come up with some very popular new dishes and sales have taken off

D Pair work. Negotiate a solution to the situation below and role-play it with your partner.

Student A: You want to go away this weekend with your friends to relax and have fun.

Student B: You are Student A's brother/sister. You want him or her to stay home and help get ready for a big family party.

Today's Workplace

Lesson B | Job choices

1 GET READY TO READ

What do you want to be when you grow up?

 When you were a child what did you want to be when you grew up? Did your ideas change?

A Children and teenagers at schools around New York City were asked by a local news magazine, "What do you want to be when you grow up?" Read what they said.

Address: http://www.localbuzz.net/teensinterview.htm

HOME | QUIZ | INTERVIEWS | LATEST | CONTACT US

What do you want to be when you grow up?

I want to be a doctor so I can help people when they are sick. Also, my mom is a doctor and I want to be like her.
— Mei Ling, 10

I haven't really thought about it. Maybe I'll do something in computer animation or game design. I just want a job that will let me get ahead and make enough money to live a good life.
— Justin, 15

I want to be an archaeologist because I like to dig things up and find things. I like adventure, too.
— Manuel, 11

I'm not really sure what I want to be yet. It's hard to know for sure what my true calling is; you know, the kind of work that I'm best suited for—something that will make me happy. Right now, I'm just trying to get into a good college. — Yoon Jin,18

I'd like to be President of the United States. There's never been a woman president. I want to be the first one.
— Emma, 8

I just took a test at school that helps you figure out what your strengths are so you know what job is right for you. My results said I ought to be an accountant or stockbroker, something like that.
— Mahesh, 17

B Pair work. **Answer the questions below with a partner.**

1. What does each young person want to be?
2. How are the responses similar?
3. How are they different?
4. Yoon Jin says, "It's hard to know for sure what my true calling is . . . " What does she mean by "true calling"?
5. Which of the others seems to know his or her true calling? Explain your answer.

C Pair work. **Do you know what your true calling is? Discuss your ideas with your partner.**

Your True Calling

A Skim the interview on page 71. Then complete the sentence below.

The interview with Cristina Resende is mainly about _____.

a. her goal to become the president of a technology company
b. her plans for traveling throughout the Mediterranean region
c. her desire to buy and run a small store in her neighborhood

B Find the information that completes these sentences.

1. Cristina believes her true calling is _____.
2. She didn't pursue this dream when she was younger because _____.
3. Cristina's current occupations are _____.
4. Cristina found out about The Mediterranean after _____.
5. Cristina was nervous the day she asked to work at The Mediterranean because _____.
6. In three months Cristina is going to _____.

C Pair work. Who do you think said each statement below? Write the person's name. Underline the information in the reading you used to make your choice. Then compare your answers with a partner.

1. __Cristina__ "The experience I've gained in the business world has prepared me to manage a store."

2. _____ "Why would you quit your job as a manager to run a deli? There's no stability in that!"

3. _____ "I know she loves food, but I wasn't sure at first why she wanted to work at The Mediterranean."

4. _____ "I'm glad that someone I trust is going to take over The Mediterranean."

5. _____ "I'm sure you'll do great! I wish I could quit my job and pursue my dream."

> **Reminder: Inferencing**
>
> Information is not always stated directly. Often a reader must infer, or make guesses about something, using the information that is available in the reading.

D Pair work. Reread the interview and find the expressions below. What do you think each one means? Write a short definition, and then compare your ideas with a partner.

1. (line 45) an opportunity in disguise _____
2. (line 48) I had butterflies in my stomach _____
3. (line 56) so to speak _____
4. (line 86) come around _____

E Pair work. Discuss the situations below with a partner.

1. Have you, or someone you know, ever been offered an opportunity in disguise?
2. Talk about a time that you had butterflies in your stomach.
3. Have you ever come around to something you didn't like at first?

> ▶ **Ask & Answer**
>
> What do you think is the best way to find your true calling in life?

Your True Calling

Do you ever find yourself thinking, "What exactly do I want to do with my life?" Tim Warner interviews Cristina Resende, a 32-year-old businesswoman who has recently found a way to pursue her true calling.

5 **Interviewer:** Why don't we start off [begin] by talking a little about how you developed your interest in food and cooking.

Resende: Well, food has always been my passion. As a child, I used to love preparing meals
10 with my grandmother, who was from Brazil. And as I got older, I spent a lot of time in the kitchen, experimenting with different dishes—Thai soups, German tortes, Italian pastas.

15 **Interviewer:** But you never considered a career in the culinary arts?

Resende: Not at all. You know, as a kid, I grew up [was raised] learning that a person went to college
20 and got a job in business, law, or something like that. Telling my parents that I wanted to "study food" would've been impossible. They never would have agreed.

Interviewer: So, fast forward to the present. You're
25 now a business development manager for an international technology company. It doesn't exactly sound like the career you dreamed of. Tell us, how did The Mediterranean come into your life?

30 **Resende:** About three years ago, I moved into an apartment around the corner from this store—it's a lovely little place that specializes in imported food from [stop by / go there] Greece, Spain, and Italy. There's a deli
35 as well. Anyway, I'd drop in there once a week or so to pick up different items. [buy / take] But the next thing you know, I was talking with the owner, Alex Kanellos, about a cheese or a certain wine. Then
40 one day, he jokingly suggested that I work in the deli since I had all of these ideas. I just laughed when he said it, but when I got home, I couldn't stop thinking that maybe this part-time job was an
45 opportunity in disguise.

Interviewer: So you took the job?

Resende: Oh yeah. I went to the deli the next morning. I had butterflies in my stomach. I kept thinking . . . I'm thirty years old and I'm taking a part-time job 50 in a deli. What am I doing? [laughs] When I asked Mr. Kanellos if he was serious about letting me work there part-time, he looked a little surprised at first. But then, Mr. Kanellos handed me 55 an apron, and the rest is history, so to speak. I've been working there every Saturday for the last couple of years.

Interviewer: What led to your decision to buy the deli?

Resende: About eight months ago, Mr. Kanellos 60 mentioned that he was getting ready to retire, and was going to sell the place. So, I started thinking . . . if he's going to sell it to someone, why not me? When I approached Mr. Kanellos with the idea, 65 he was very open to it. I also think he was pleased to turn over the place to [change ownership / give] someone he knew.

Interviewer: And what about your job with the tech company? 70

Resende: I'm going to stay for another three months, until Mr. Kanellos retires.

Interviewer: How are your family and friends reacting to the news?

Resende: My friends are really happy for me. A lot 75 of them have jobs they can't stand—especially my friend Suki—and most would love to make a change in their lives. My boyfriend has been pretty supportive, too, though at first, he 80 thought I was crazy to work part-time at the deli. My mom isn't thrilled, though. She's worried about me leaving a "good job" to run the store, but I know that as a small businesswoman, I can be 85 successful, too. I'm sure she'll come around! [change opinion]

your pet's pur

Applying for a job

A Pair work. **Read the job listing and then the cover letter below. Discuss with your partner why Dale Sanford thinks he is qualified for the job.**

Animal care specialist

National Zoo requires experienced person to feed, water, and clean the cages of small animals. Duties also include conducting tours for young visitors. Send résumé and cover letter to Cassandra Beck, National Zoo, P.O. Box 42, Metropolis City MA 02210

980 Wilson Drive
Metropolis City MA 02203

Ms. Cassandra Beck
National Zoo
P.O. Box 42
Metropolis City MA 02210

Dear Ms. Beck:

I'm writing to apply for the position that was advertised in the Metropolis Daily News. My background makes me very well-qualified to be an animal care specialist. I will graduate next month from Pacific University with a degree in biology and have taken several courses in animal behavior. During my summer vacations, I worked in the office of a local veterinarian and helped to care for a variety of animals, including dogs, cats, snakes, and birds. I am also a volunteer for Save the Animals, a local rescue group. My own pets include two dogs, a rabbit, and a turtle, all adopted through Save the Animals. My résumé is enclosed. Thank you very much for your consideration, and I look forward to hearing from you.

Sincerely,
Dale Sanford
Dale Sanford

B Pair work. **In the body of the letter, underline the purpose of the letter. Circle Dale's qualifications for the job. Then discuss these questions with a partner.**

1. What information is included in the first sentence of the letter?
2. Do you think Dale is qualified for the job?

C **Choose one of the job listings below and write a cover letter to apply for the job. Include your purpose for writing the letter and at least three qualifications that make you right for the job.**

International Tour Guide Tour leaders needed for our small-group luxury tours to Hawaii, South America, and East Asia. Excellent salary and benefits, plus unlimited free travel. Contact Melinda Lee, Starline Travel, 16 Bayfield Drive, Mayfield, NY 22267

Personal shopper Gracy's Department Store is looking for people with a great sense of style to help our customers plan their wardrobes. Competitive salary plus great employee discounts on all our clothes. Contact Personnel Dept., P.O. Box 401, San Francisco CA 61240

D Pair work. **Exchange letters with a partner. Make two suggestions to improve your partner's letter.**

Activity 1: Appointment with a career counselor

A Pair work. **Interview your partner using the questions below.**

1. What are (or were) your favorite subjects in school? _____

2. What are three things that really make you happy? _____

3. What skills or talents do you have? What things are you good at doing? List at least two.

   _____   _____

4. How would you finish this sentence?

   I prefer to . . .

   ☐ work on my own.   ☐ work as a member of a team.   ☐ manage a group of people.

5. What is most important to you in a career? Rank each of the following from 1 to 3.

   (1 = not important   2 = somewhat important   3 = very important)

   ☐ money   ☐ freedom to be my own boss

   ☐ intellectual challenge   ☐ helping others

   ☐ a flexible schedule   ☐ company perks (e.g., gym membership, day care for children)

   ☐ a good retirement package   ☐ a creative environment

   ☐ the ability to travel   ☐ other _____

B Pair work. **Look at the answers your partner gave you in** A. **What career(s) do you think your partner is best suited for? Why? Choose from the list below or come up with your own ideas.**

tour guide	DJ	yoga instructor	professional shopper	firefighter	doctor or nurse
decorator	lawyer	private investigator	scientist	chef	carpenter
engineer	taxi driver	game programmer	jewelry designer	coach	editor

Activity 2: Try to see things my way

A Pair work. **Assume one of the roles below. With your partner, try to reach an agreement about what to do by the end of your conversation.**

Student A: You're a senior in college majoring in business. You've decided to give up your studies and drop out of school to pursue your true calling in life, which you believe is a career in music. To begin your new life as a musician, you need to borrow some money. You decide to talk to a parent. Explain your plans and try to get your parent to come around to your way of thinking.

Student B: You're Student A's parent. You are against your child's plans. You think your son or daughter is making a very serious mistake and is going to throw his or her life away by dropping out of school and becoming a musician. You think your child should complete his or her studies and put off doing anything in music until after graduation.

B Group work. **Perform your role play for another pair.**

 **Check out the CNN® video.**   **Practice your English online at** <u>elt.heinle.com/worldpass</u>

Unit 6: Today's Workplace

A Study the word combinations in the box. Then complete the sentences, using the correct form of the phrase.

> **More word combinations with *get***
>
> *get off* = leave from work; be released from something without penalty
> *get into* = become involved in; enter
> *get behind* = support
> *get around* = avoid (usually doing something)
> *get around to* = do something eventually, often after procrastinating
> *get along with* = be compatible with
> *get together* = meet informally

1. Let's get _____ at the coffee shop some time next week, OK?
2. In her speech, the mayor urged citizens to get _____ the city's clean-up campaign.
3. I got _____ holiday crowds last year by ordering presents over the Internet.
4. Kayla got _____ surfing while she was on vacation in Hawaii. She loves it.
5. I'd always wanted to plant a garden, and I finally got _____ it last year.
6. Ray just doesn't get _____ his boss. They argue a lot.
7. Would you like to meet me after work? I get _____ at 6:30 tonight.

B Circle the term that doesn't fit. Use your dictionary as necessary.

1. salary   wages   paycheck   bills
2. boss   supervisor   intern   manager
3. out of work   layoff   unemployed   take off
4. application   calling   ambition   goal
5. get ahead   successful   profitable   go under
6. come up with   invent   give up   make
7. career   customer   job   position
8. give up   stick with   continue   keep on

> **I didn't know that!**
> In ancient Rome, soldiers received a handful of salt every day to use on their food. After a while, this was replaced by money to buy salt. The payment was called *salarium* in Latin (meaning "salt money").
> Later, in several European languages, *salary* became a word for any kind of pay for work.

C Match these sentences with their uses.

1. Everything will work out. ___
2. Get to work! ___
3. We can work it out. ___
4. You have your work cut out for you. ___
5. It's in the works. ___
6. Don't get all worked up about it. (informal) ___

a. used to say that people can make an agreement
b. used to say that a project will be very difficult
c. used to tell someone not to get upset about something
d. used to say that a situation will be OK
e. used to tell someone to stop being lazy
f. used to say that something is being planned or prepared

D Complete the conversations with one of the sentences from C.

1. A: Mom, why are you yelling at me?
   B: I told you to clean your room, but you haven't. _____!

2. A: Maybe we should break up . . . I love you, but we just argue all the time.
   B: But I don't want to stop seeing you! _____.

3. A: What are we going to have to eat at our party? I don't have any time to cook!
   B: Don't worry. I asked everyone to bring snacks. _____.

4. A: Julio said he would call me last night, and I waited up until midnight!
   B: _____. He probably just forgot.

5. A: I'm going to be designing and maintaining the company's new web site.
   B: Wow, _____! That's a big job.

6. A: When will you be transferred to the New York office?
   B: I'm not sure yet, but my boss told me _____.

E What do these scientists study? Match the columns. Then circle the job that would be most interesting for you.

1. An oceanographer studies ____.   a. plants
2. An astronomer studies ____.   b. animals
3. A psychologist studies ____.   c. ancient civilizations
4. A meteorologist studies ____.   d. the weather
5. A zoologist studies ____.   e. the sea
6. A botanist studies ____.   f. the earth and rocks
7. A geologist studies ____.   g. the human mind
8. An archaeologist studies ____.   h. space

In Other Words

Company is a general term for a business organization that makes or sells things: *Sony is a Japanese company.*
A business can be large or small: *My sister has her own business—she's a hairdresser.*
A firm is a business of professionals: *Claudia works for a big accounting firm.*
A corporation is a large business with special legal status: *I have fifty shares of stock in that corporation.*

To succeed means to achieve your goals: *Her ambition was to become a pilot, and she succeeded.*
Make it is an informal expression for succeed in a profession: *It's really hard to make it as a new actor in Hollywood.*
If you are doing well, you are successful in work or education: *My brother's company is doing very well. / My son is studying at Oxford University, and he's doing very well.*
If you thrive on something, it motivates or energizes you to succeed: *Athletes thrive on competition.*

staff
Staff is a collective noun (similar to *team, faculty,* or *family*). It refers to the whole group of workers and is uncountable. To refer to one person, use *staff member.*
   Our company sent three staff members to the conference.
   Our company sent three ~~staffs~~ to the conference.

Review: Units 4–6

1 LANGUAGE CHECK

Circle the correct answer.

1. Last year, I didn't have my driver's license yet,
   so I _____ drive my dad's new car.
   a. mustn't   b. couldn't   c. didn't have to

2. It's raining hard. Let's put ___ the picnic until next week.
   a. up   b. off   c. in

3. The car was completely destroyed in the crash.
   The driver _____ been going very fast.
   a. must have   b. can't have   c. may not have

4. I came up ___ a great idea for redecorating my living room.
   a. over   b. with   c. across

5. I waited for an hour, but my friends didn't show up.
   I think I _____ made a mistake about the date.
   a. couldn't have   b. should have   c. may have

6. Dina didn't study but she got a good grade.
   That class _____ been very difficult!
   a. must have   b. might have   c. couldn't have

7. In my opinion, if you like Denise,
   you _____ call her and ask her out on a date.
   a. could   b. should   c. must

8. I brought a raincoat and an umbrella with me,
   but the weather was good, so I _____ use them.
   a. was required to   b. didn't have to   c. wasn't permitted to

9. I didn't hear my cell phone ring. I ___ turned it on.
   a. must not have   b. could have   c. should not have

10. I stayed up all night working, and I handed
    ___ my report to my professor today.
    a. in   b. out   c. ahead

11. During the exam, we were _____ to put all our books
    and papers on the floor.
    a. chosen   b. required   c. needed

12. You have to work really hard if you want to get
    _____ in the software industry.
    a. ahead   b. over   c. about

2 VOCABULARY CHECK

Complete the sentences with words from the box, adding articles (*a, an*) as necessary. You will NOT use all of the words.

incident	theory	visionary	seemingly	evidence	documents
generation	witness	circumstances	apathetic	issue	motivated

1. Many people in the _____ born after 1990
   don't know life without the Internet.

2. Don't be so _____ about global warming!
   If we don't take action, every living thing could be
   harmed.

3. Scientists have _____ that the dinosaurs
   died out because of climate change.

4. Improving public transportation is an important
   _____ in my city.

5. There is no _____ that Jim Thompson was
   eaten by a jungle tiger.

6. Many young people are very _____ and
   really work to improve the world we live in.

7. Investigators found a box of _____ that
   showed that the bank president had been stealing
   money from customers' accounts.

8. Older people in my country grew up in very different
   _____. The roads were poor and
   communication was difficult.

9. The new president is facing a _____
   impossible task: reducing the high rate of
   unemployment in the country.

10. There was _____ in which two boys
    started fighting in the classroom.

Situation 1

Situation 2

Situation 3

A Pair work. Choose one of the pictures and imagine yourselves in the situation. What would the people talk about? Briefly review the language notes from Units 4–6.

B Pair work. Read the statements in C and add two of your own goals. Then role-play the situation you chose keeping your speaking goals in mind.

C Now rate your speaking. Use + for good, ✓ for OK, and – for things you need to improve.

How did you do?	
I spoke loudly enough for my partner(s) to hear me.	
I spoke without too much hesitation.	
I spoke at a good rate of speed—not too fast or too slow.	
I used new vocabulary from the units.	
I used at least three expressions from the units.	
I practiced the grammar from the units.	
My own goals: 1. _____ 2. _____	

WORLD PASS

Expanding English Fluency

Susan Stempleski
James R. Morgan
Nancy Douglas
Kristin L. Johannsen

HEINLE
CENGAGE Learning·

Australia · Brazil · Japan · Korea · Mexico · Singapore · Spain · United Kingdom · United States

World Pass Upper-Intermediate,
Combo Split A
Susan Stempleski
James R. Morgan, Nancy Douglas,
Kristin L. Johannsen

Publisher: Christopher Wenger
Director of Content Development:
Anita Raducanu
Director of Product Marketing: Amy Mabley
Acquisitions Editor: Mary Sutton-Paul
Sr. Marketing Manager: Rebbecca Klevberg
Content Project Manager: Tan Jin Hock
Sr. Print Buyer: Mary Beth Hennebury
International Marketing Manager:
Ian Martin
Contributing Development Editor:
Paul MacIntyre
Compositor: Parkwood Composition Service
Photo Researcher: Christopher Hanzie
Illustrator: Ray Medici
Cover/Text Designer: Christopher Hanzie,
CHROME Media Pte. Ltd.
Photo Credits
5: © The Photolibrary Wales/Alamy; 10: top to bottom: Photos.com/
RF, © Royalty-Free/Corbis, Photos.com/RF, Photos.com/RF,
24: Index Open/RF; 28: © Yann Arthus-Bertrand/CORBIS; 29: ©
BennettPhoto/Alamy; 30: Photos.com/RF; 31: Photos.com/RF;

ISBN-13: 978-1-4130-1088-6

ISBN-10: 1-4130-1088-1

Heinle
25 Thomson Place
Boston, Massachusetts 02210
USA

Cengage Learning is a leading provider of customized learning solutions with office locations around the globe, including Singapore, the United Kingdom, Australia, Mexico, Brazil and Japan. Locate our local office at:
international.cengage.com/region

Cengage Learning products are represented in Canada by Nelson Education, Ltd.

Visit Heinle online at **elt.heinle.com**
Visit our corporate website at **cengage.com**

Combo Split A

Scope and Sequence

What's the Story?

Lesson A | The story of my life

1 VOCABULARY & EXPRESSIONS

A Complete the sentences with verbs from the box. Be sure to use the correct tense.

verify	make up	alter	go after
go over	interpret	piece together	cover

1. The teenager confessed that he _____ the story about the car being stolen. He had gotten in an accident and was afraid his father would get angry with him.

2. It took months of work for reporters to _____ the story of how a secretary stole millions of dollars from the bank.

3. Liza is a journalist who _____ stories on technology for *Business 2000* magazine.

4. The newspaper reporter couldn't _____ the story about the tiger that was seen walking around the suburbs. It was just a rumor.

5. You can _____ news stories about developing countries in different ways. Some people think things are getting better, other people disagree.

6. The witness to the bank robbery _____ her story. She said she'd made a mistake, and there were three robbers, not two.

7. Editors always _____ a story before it appears in the newspaper to check all the facts and statistics.

8. It took a lot of courage for those reporters to _____ the story about drug smugglers.

B Think of an interesting experience that you, or someone you know, had. Complete the sentences to tell the story.

1. Did I ever tell you about the time when _____?

2. It happened when _____.

3. I think it was about _____ years/months/days ago.

4. It began when _____.

5. Then _____

_____

_____

6. In the end, _____.

7. Looking back on it, _____

_____

2 GRAMMAR

A Read the e-mail and fill in the correct form of the verb, simple past or present perfect.

IN

Reply   Forward   Delete   New   Get Mail   Trash

You have new mail!

From: cjr5303@uni.edu
To: suarez@wowmail.net
Subj: This week's news

Hi Mom,

Sorry I (1. write, not) _didn't write_ to you last week—I just (2. have, not) _didn't have_ time then. I (3. be) _have been_ so busy with my classes this semester. Since the beginning of the term, I (4. have) _have had_ a test in every class, and I (5. spend) _have spent_ almost every evening this week studying in the library.

Last weekend, I (6. do) _did_ something fun, though. I (7. go) _went_ on a hike with the University Outdoor Club. We (8. take) _took_ a bus out to the mountains, (9. climb) _climbed_ White Peak, and (10. cook) _cooked_ lunch at the top. It (11. feel) _felt_ great to be outside and away from my books! I (12. get, not) _haven't gotten_ much exercise since I came here—I know I need more.

I (13. make, not) _haven't made_ my plane reservations for winter vacation yet, but I'll do that this week. It will be great to see everyone—I can't believe it (14. be) _has been_ five months already!

Love, Carmen

B Write questions for these answers.

1. Q1: _What did you do yesterday?_ ?
   A: I ran in a marathon.
   Q2: _What have you done all day today?_ ?
   A: I've run in a marathon.

2. Q1: _Where did your friends live last year_ ?
   A: They lived in Mexico and Guatemala.
   Q2: _Where have your friends lived this year_ ?
   A: They've lived in Mexico and Guatemala.

3. Q1: _What did your sister do last year_ ?
   A: She worked in a restaurant as a cook.
   Q2: _What has your sister done this year_ ?
   A: She's worked in a restaurant as a cook.

C Answer the questions.

1. What's something you've never done that you'd like to try? Why?
   To go to Las vegas for the casino. because I'm afraid of it a little

2. What's something you've done that you never want to do again? Why?

Lesson A • The story of my life   **3**

What's the Story?

| **Lesson B** | Tell me a story. |

A Before reading

1. What are some famous old folk stories from your country? _____

_____

2. How did you first learn these stories? _____

_____

3. Which is more fun, reading a story or hearing it? Why? _____

_____

B Read the article and fill in the interview questions in the correct spaces.

a. How can I tell stories better?

b. Where do you find your stories?

c. What, exactly, do professional storytellers do?

d. Do you have to do anything special to take care of your voice?

e. Where do you tell your stories?

f. How did you become a professional storyteller? Is there a story behind that?

g. What happens at a storytelling festival?

The Art of the Story
by Mina Desai

Storytelling is an ancient art that is practiced in every country around the world. In the United States, Canada, Australia, and other countries, people gather at storytelling festivals to hear performers in costume tell stories that are old favorites—and new ones you've never heard before. There are even professional storytellers, like Douglas MacGregor, who puts on more than 150 shows a year. I spoke with him after a recent performance at the National Theater.

1. Interviewer: _____?

We're artists who tell all sorts of stories, from traditional folk tales, to urban tales, to personal stories, to business stories. And we all do it in our own way. There are some traditional storytellers who entertain people using only their words and voice. Other storytellers like to add movement, music, **props**, and costumes to **enhance** their stories.

2. Interviewer: _____?

Most of my performances are in the field of education—at schools and libraries. I also appear at children's parties, and festivals like the National Storytelling Festival in the USA, and the Yukon Storytelling Festival in Canada. I generally do about 150 shows a year.

3. Interviewer: _____?

Oh, it's **tremendous** fun! Usually they last several days, and there are performers from a number of countries, and everyone sits in a huge tent and listens to the most wonderful stories, from morning till night.

4. Interviewer: _____?

A lot of them are traditional English and Scottish stories that I first heard from my grandparents, but I always try to adapt them to the audience. Others come from very old children's books. And some of them are rooted in my own personal experiences. Of course, nowadays there are hundreds of websites with story collections.

5. Interviewer: _____?

I try to rest it as much as I can, and I take plenty of vitamin C and **herbs**. Of course, alcohol, tobacco, and caffeine are all damaging, so I avoid them . . . when I can!

6. Interviewer: _____?

First, relax! People just want to have fun listening to your story. Tell the story in your own words—don't try to memorize it. If you **get stuck** and can't remember the next part, just keep talking about the part you remember, and add more sensory details—for example, what color was the house? What did it look like, exactly? And finally, keep your stories under ten minutes.

7. Interviewer: _____?

Yes, indeed! Once upon a time, there was a young man who wanted to tell stories . . .

C Circle *T* for true, *F* for false, or *NI* for no information.

1. MacGregor performs mainly in theaters. T F NI

2. Storytelling festivals are held on weekends. T F NI

3. MacGregor's grandparents knew a lot of stories. T F NI

4. Good stories shouldn't be too long. T F NI

5. Tea is good for your voice. T F NI

6. MacGregor sometimes tells stories about himself. T F NI

7. The stories at festivals must be traditional. T F NI

8. McGregor took a special course to learn storytelling. T F NI

D Look at the words from the article in bold. Choose the correct answer by thinking about the context of the word.

1. **Props** are probably _____ used in a theater.
   a. seats b. clothes c. objects

2. **Enhance** probably means _____.
   a. make shorter b. modernize c. improve

3. **Tremendous** probably means _____.
   a. great b. possible c. expensive

4. **Herbs** are probably _____.
   a. medicinal plants b. alcoholic drinks c. sweet foods

5. If you **get stuck**, you can't _____.
   a. stop b. go on c. understand

A paragraph is a short piece of writing that focuses on one idea. A paragraph usually has three parts: a topic sentence that tells you the main idea of the paragraph, supporting sentences that explain the idea, and a conclusion sentence that summarizes the idea.

A Read these paragraphs. Underline the topic sentence in each, and list the supporting details (short notes only). Circle the conclusion sentence.

---

1. The Value of Gold

There are three reasons why gold is so valuable. First, it is beautiful. People in virtually every culture have used it in jewelry and works of art. Second, it is useful. It conducts electricity well, and many electronic devices contain small amounts of gold. Finally, it is scarce. It occurs in few places in the world, and often many tons of rock must be processed to remove just a few grams of gold. For these reasons, the price of gold is always high.

Supporting details:

a. _____

b. _____

c. _____

---

2. Arabic: A World Language

Arabic is one of the world's major languages. More than 200 million people in countries from Morocco to Saudi Arabia speak it. For Muslims, it is the language of their religion and their holy book. Arabic writing is used by 15 percent of the world's people, and millions of people in Asia and Africa write their own languages using the Arabic alphabet. In the future, the Arabic language is likely to become even more important.

Supporting details:

a. _____   c. _____

b. _____   d. _____

---

3. Gorillas of the Rainforest

Gorillas are among the largest, most powerful animals in the African rainforest. An adult male gorilla can reach 180 cm in height. Some of the heaviest gorillas weigh over 200 kg. They are extremely strong, although they are generally peace-loving and fight very little. The destruction of their rainforest habitat means that these animals are now endangered by humans.

Supporting details:

a. _____

b. _____

c. _____

B Look at the format of the paragraphs and answer the questions.

1. Where is the title of the paragraph? _____

2. Which words in the title have capital letters? _____

3. Where is the beginning of the first sentence in relation to the margin? _____
_____

4. Where is the beginning of all the other sentences? _____
_____

Writing is easier if you take some time to think and plan first. Start by making short notes of your ideas.

C Choose a memorable experience that you've had and complete this topic sentence:

I once had a very unusual/funny/sad/_____ experience.

What are some words and ideas you could use in your paragraph? (You do NOT need complete sentences.)

_____   _____

_____   _____

_____   _____

_____   _____

_____   _____

D Now write your paragraph, following the correct format. Use these expressions to show the time order of the events in your story.

First (off),	Next,	Then,	Later,	Before
The next day,	Two months later,	Finally,	In the end,	After

_____

_____

_____

_____

_____

_____

_____

_____

_____

_____

_____

_____

_____

_____

_____

Lesson A | Technostress

---

1 VOCABULARY & EXPRESSIONS

A Fill in the spaces with words from the box.

> interaction   recipe for disaster   multitasking   impersonal   information overload
> sedentary   overdependence   liberating   promote

Technostress is becoming a serious problem in many large companies. Too many employees spend their whole day **(1)** _____, answering the phone while they check their e-mail in the middle of writing a report. It's almost impossible for them to deal with the **(2)** _____ of papers, websites, and reports they are required to read. In addition, too many office workers are completely **(3)** _____ and spend up to ten hours a day sitting. In the past, there was more **(4)** _____ with colleagues, because employees would meet together to work on projects. In the last few years, work has become more **(5)** _____, and many projects are done at a distance through e-mail and the Internet.

Some experts say this situation is a **(6)** _____, and many employees will develop work-related health problems. They say that companies need to end their **(7)** _____ on technology, and use it only when really necessary. By **(8)** _____ their employees from technostress, companies will improve their business, and also **(9)** _____ good health among their workers.

B Answer the questions.

1. When do you use multitasking? _____

   _____

2. Do you suffer from technostress? Explain your answer. _____

   _____

3. What's something that you're overdependent on? Why? _____

   _____

C Complete the chart with information about yourself.

I'm pretty good at . . .	I'm no good at . . .	I know something about . . .	I haven't got a clue about . . .

2 GRAMMAR

A Label these sentences *active* or *passive*.

1. The new city hall building was completed in 2001. _____

2. Andre was very happy about getting a promotion at work. _____

3. Rice is grown in many Asian countries. _____

4. The first computers in the 1940s were quite large. _____

5. Potatoes are an important food in many European countries. _____

6. Many people think the Taj Mahal is the world's most beautiful building. _____

7. The Pyramids were surrounded by other buildings in ancient times. _____

8. Temperatures are measured with two different systems, Celsius and Fahrenheit. _____

9. The basketball players were tired after practicing for three hours. _____

10. The stolen jewels were found after a long search. _____

5/25
(H.W)

B Rewrite these sentences in the passive voice.

1. Professors at a famous university wrote that book. *Who was the book written by?*
   That book was written by professors at a famous university.

2. Over ten thousand people attended the soccer match.
   The soccer match was attended by over ten thousand people.

3. Several companies produce electric cars.
   Electric cars are produced by several companies.

4. The president didn't answer the journalists' questions. *Who were the journalists' questions answered by?*
   The journalists' questions weren't answered by the president.

5. The police arrested several dangerous criminals.
   Several dangerous criminals were arrested by the police.

6. The government is building many new schools. *Who are many new schools **being** built by?*
   *Many new schools are **being built**ng by the government.*

7. The bad news didn't surprise me. *What was I surprised by?* • *where is christmas celebrated in summer?*
   I wasn't surprised by the bad news.

8. People in Australia celebrate Christmas in summer. *When is Christmas celebrated in Australia?*
   Christmas in summer is celebrated by people in Australia.

C Write passive sentences about the items in the picture. Use a different verb in each sentence.

1. _____

2. _____

3. _____

4. _____

Products of **EUROPE**

Germany
Italy
Switzerland
France

Accidental Technology

(1) An old proverb says that "Necessity is the mother of invention"—meaning that when people need something, they find a way to do it. But if you look at real-life stories of technology, you'll see that not all inventions were planned. Some of them were accidents—or even mistakes!

(2) In the 1940s, a scientist named Percy Spencer was working to develop radar systems for the U.S. military. One day, in his laboratory, he noticed that a chocolate bar in his pocket had gotten very soft and melted—even though it wasn't hot in the room. He was standing next to a machine called a magnetron. Quickly, he did an experiment, putting some kernels of corn next to the magnetron. In a minute, he had popcorn. And that was how the microwave oven was invented.

(3) On a sunny day in 1948, a Swiss man named George de Mestral decided to take his dog out for a walk in the forest. When they got home, the dog's fur was full of seeds that were practically impossible to remove. The seeds were also sticking to Mestral's pants. Curious, he took one of the seeds and looked at it under the microscope. There, he saw that the seeds were covered with tiny hooks that stuck to animal's fur—and people's pants. He used this principle to develop the Velcro fasteners that are used on everyday items like shoes, clothing, and backpacks.

(4) Some very useful inventions started as failures. Spence Silver was trying to create an extra-strong kind of glue for an American company, but the glue that he produced didn't work at all. It couldn't even hold two pieces of paper together—they came apart when you pulled on them. He gave up on the super-glue, and turned to other projects. Then, several years later, one of his colleagues, Art Fry, was singing in church one Sunday. The slips of paper that he used to mark his place in the songbook often fell out, and he got an idea. Perhaps Silver's glue could solve the problem? Together, they went on to develop Post-It notes, which were first sold in 1979.

(5) "Accidental inventions" have been happening for a long time. In 1839, a salesman was experimenting with a new product from Brazil called rubber. It could be used to make erasers, but it melted at high temperatures, and broke when it was cold. The inventor tried mixing it with different chemicals, but nothing worked—until he accidentally dropped it on a hot stove. Heat made the rubber strong and flexible, in a process called vulcanization. Thanks to Charles Goodyear's accident, we now have rubber tires for our cars, and rubber soles for our shoes.

5/27

B Complete the chart with information from the reading.

Name(s)	Charles Goodyear	Percy Spencer	Spence Silver and Art Fry	George de Mestral
Invention	Valcanized rubber	microwave	post-it	Velcro
Year	1839	1940s	1979	1948
How it was invented	dropped rubber on a hot stove	put kernels of corn next to the magnetron.	papers fell out of his songbook	The sees were sticked to pants.
Uses	cars, rubber soles for our shoes	cooking food	mark his place in the book	Shoes, clothing, backpacks.

C Look back through the reading and find words with these meanings in the paragraphs indicated.

1. needing (par. 1) _necessity_
2. seeds (par. 2) _kernels_
3. animal hair (par.3) _fur_
4. almost (par.3) _practically_
5. things used to keep other things closed (par. 3) _fasten (v.) (n.) fastener_
6. small pieces of paper (par. 4) _slips of paper_
7. easy to bend (par. 5) _flexible_

' hologram
' 3-dimensional image

D Answer the questions.

1. Which of these inventions is the most important in your life? Why? _____

2. What other inventions do you rely on in your everyday life? _____

3. What is an important invention that we need now? Why? _____

Every paragraph needs a strong topic sentence. The topic sentence contains two things: the topic (what your paragraph is about) and the controlling idea (your idea or attitude about this topic).

A In each of these topic sentences, circle the topic and underline the controlling idea.

Example: Drinking (coffee) can have several <u>negative effects</u> on your health.

1. Instant messaging has made my daily life much easier.

2. One reason I admire my grandmother is because she is so generous.

3. In my country, university entrance exams are a stressful experience for students.

4. A camping trip is the most relaxing kind of vacation.

5. Air pollution is causing serious problems for the people of my city.

6. My first day at my new job was not easy for me.

B Choose the best topic sentence for each paragraph and write it on the line.

1. _____

In winter, the weather is usually sunny and pleasant. Nights are cool, but the daytime is warm. Most of the rain that we receive falls in January and February, and after a rainstorm, the desert turns green and flowers bloom. The weather for sightseeing and taking pictures is perfect from November to March.

    a. My country gets the most rain in January and February.
    b. Winter is the best time to visit my country.
    c. Tourists don't like to come to my country in summer.

2. _____

The English word *camel* comes from the Arabic word for the animal. *Giraffe* comes from the Arabic words for "long neck." *Zebra* comes to us from the Italian language. The ancient Greeks gave us the words *rhinoceros* and *hippopotamus,* and *leopard* came from Latin.

    a. English animal names came from many different languages.
    b. Some animals have very unusual names in English.
    c. A number of common English words originally came from Arabic.

3. _____

More than 10 million people live in and around Paris. The nation's railroad system and many major highways are centered on the city, and there are also two international airports. Paris is the center of French banking and finance, and many companies have their main offices there. Finally, it is also the site of the country's most respected universities.

    a. Paris is one of the oldest cities in Europe.
    b. Tourists love Paris because it's such a romantic city.
    c. Paris is the most important city in France.

4. _____

For one thing, a newspaper article contains a lot more information than a short TV news report. You can understand world events much better. Furthermore, I can read the newspaper whenever I have a few minutes— on the subway, during my coffee break at work, or even in the bathtub. Finally, I can choose only the articles I'm really interested in, instead of having to watch all the boring TV news stories on things I don't care about. That's why I read the newspaper every day.

    a. TV news programs are more popular than newspapers.
    b. News events can have a big impact on our daily lives.
    c. Newspapers have several advantages over TV news programs.

2 GRAMMAR

A Label these sentences *active* or *passive*.

1. The new city hall building was completed in 2001. _____

2. Andre was very happy about getting a promotion at work. _____

3. Rice is grown in many Asian countries. _____

4. The first computers in the 1940s were quite large. _____

5. Potatoes are an important food in many European countries. _____

6. Many people think the Taj Mahal is the world's most beautiful building. _____

7. The Pyramids were surrounded by other buildings in ancient times. _____

8. Temperatures are measured with two different systems, Celsius and Fahrenheit. _____

9. The basketball players were tired after practicing for three hours. _____

10. The stolen jewels were found after a long search. _____

5/25
(H.W)

B Rewrite these sentences in the passive voice.

1. Professors at a famous university wrote that book.
Who was the book written by?
That book was written by professors at a famous university.

2. Over ten thousand people attended the soccer match.
The soccer match was attended by over ten thousand people.

3. Several companies produce electric cars.
Electric cars are produced by several companies.

4. The president didn't answer the journalists' questions. *Who were the journalists' questions answered*
The journalists' questions weren't answered by the *by?*
president.

5. The police arrested several dangerous criminals.
Several dangerous criminals were arrested by the police

6. The government is building many new schools. *Who are many new schools being built by?*
Many new schools are being built ng by the government.

7. The bad news didn't surprise me. *What was I surprised by?* *where is christmas*
I wasn't surprised by the bad news. *celebrated in summer?*

8. People in Australia celebrate Christmas in summer. *When is Christmas celebrated in Australia?*
Christmas in summer is celebrated by people in Australia.

C Write passive sentences about the items in the picture. Use a different verb in each sentence.

1. _____

2. _____

3. _____

4. _____

Products of EUROPE

Germany

Italy

Switzerland

France

Technology

5/26

| **Lesson B** | Techno-shopping |

1 READING

A Read this magazine article about advances in technology.

Accidental Technology

① An old proverb says that "Necessity is the mother of invention"—meaning that when people need something, they find a way to do it. But if you look at real-life stories of technology, you'll see that not all inventions were planned. Some of them were accidents—or even mistakes!

② In the 1940s, a scientist named Percy Spencer was working to develop radar systems for the U.S. military. One day, in his laboratory, he noticed that a chocolate bar in his pocket had gotten very soft and melted—even though it wasn't hot in the room. He was standing next to a machine called a magnetron. Quickly, he did an experiment, putting some kernels of corn next to the magnetron. In a minute, he had popcorn. And that was how the microwave oven was invented.

③ On a sunny day in 1948, a Swiss man named George de Mestral decided to take his dog out for a walk in the forest. When they got home, the dog's fur was full of seeds that were practically impossible to remove. The seeds were also sticking to Mestral's pants. Curious, he took one of the seeds and looked at it under the microscope. There, he saw that the seeds were covered with tiny hooks that stuck to animal's fur—and people's pants. He used this principle to develop the Velcro fasteners that are used on everyday items like shoes, clothing, and backpacks.

④ Some very useful inventions started as failures. Spence Silver was trying to create an extra-strong kind of glue for an American company, but the glue that he produced didn't work at all. It couldn't even hold two pieces of paper together—they came apart when you pulled on them. He gave up on the super-glue, and turned to other projects. Then, several years later, one of his colleagues, Art Fry, was singing in church one Sunday. The slips of paper that he used to mark his place in the songbook often fell out, and he got an idea. Perhaps Silver's glue could solve the problem? Together, they went on to develop Post-It notes, which were first sold in 1979.

⑤ "Accidental inventions" have been happening for a long time. In 1839, a salesman was experimenting with a new product from Brazil called rubber. It could be used to make erasers, but it melted at high temperatures, and broke when it was cold. The inventor tried mixing it with different chemicals, but nothing worked—until he accidentally dropped it on a hot stove. Heat made the rubber strong and flexible, in a process called vulcanization. Thanks to Charles Goodyear's accident, we now have rubber tires for our cars, and rubber soles for our shoes.

5/27

B Complete the chart with information from the reading.

Name(s)	Charles Goodyear	Percy Spencer	Spence Silver and Art Fry	George de Mestral
Invention	Valcanized rubber	microwave	post-it	Velcro
Year	1839	1940s	1979	1948
How it was invented	dropped rubber on a hot stove	put kernels of corn next to the magnetron.	papers fell out of his songbook	The sees were sticked to pants.
Uses	cars, rubber soles for our shoes	cooking food	mark his place in the book	Shoes, clothing backpacks

C Look back through the reading and find words with these meanings in the paragraphs indicated.

1. needing (par. 1) necessity
2. seeds (par. 2) kernels
3. animal hair (par.3) fur
4. almost (par.3) practically
5. things used to keep other things closed (par. 3) fasten (v.) (n.) fastener
6. small pieces of paper (par. 4) slips of paper
7. easy to bend (par. 5) flexible

· hologram
· 3-dimensional image

D Answer the questions.

1. Which of these inventions is the most important in your life? Why? _____

2. What other inventions do you rely on in your everyday life? _____

3. What is an important invention that we need now? Why? _____

> Every paragraph needs a strong topic sentence. The topic sentence contains two things: the topic (what your paragraph is about) and the controlling idea (your idea or attitude about this topic).

A   In each of these topic sentences, circle the topic and underline the controlling idea.

Example: Drinking (coffee) can have several underline{negative effects} on your health.

1. Instant messaging has made my daily life much easier.

2. One reason I admire my grandmother is because she is so generous.

3. In my country, university entrance exams are a stressful experience for students.

4. A camping trip is the most relaxing kind of vacation.

5. Air pollution is causing serious problems for the people of my city.

6. My first day at my new job was not easy for me.

B   Choose the best topic sentence for each paragraph and write it on the line.

1. _____

In winter, the weather is usually sunny and pleasant. Nights are cool, but the daytime is warm. Most of the rain that we receive falls in January and February, and after a rainstorm, the desert turns green and flowers bloom. The weather for sightseeing and taking pictures is perfect from November to March.

    a. My country gets the most rain in January and February.
    b. Winter is the best time to visit my country.
    c. Tourists don't like to come to my country in summer.

2. _____

The English word *camel* comes from the Arabic word for the animal. *Giraffe* comes from the Arabic words for "long neck." *Zebra* comes to us from the Italian language. The ancient Greeks gave us the words *rhinoceros* and *hippopotamus,* and *leopard* came from Latin.

    a. English animal names came from many different languages.
    b. Some animals have very unusual names in English.
    c. A number of common English words originally came from Arabic.

3. _____

More than 10 million people live in and around Paris. The nation's railroad system and many major highways are centered on the city, and there are also two international airports. Paris is the center of French banking and finance, and many companies have their main offices there. Finally, it is also the site of the country's most respected universities.

    a. Paris is one of the oldest cities in Europe.
    b. Tourists love Paris because it's such a romantic city.
    c. Paris is the most important city in France.

4. _____

For one thing, a newspaper article contains a lot more information than a short TV news report. You can understand world events much better. Furthermore, I can read the newspaper whenever I have a few minutes— on the subway, during my coffee break at work, or even in the bathtub. Finally, I can choose only the articles I'm really interested in, instead of having to watch all the boring TV news stories on things I don't care about. That's why I read the newspaper every day.

    a. TV news programs are more popular than newspapers.
    b. News events can have a big impact on our daily lives.
    c. Newspapers have several advantages over TV news programs.

C Choose one of these kinds of technology to write a paragraph about and circle it.

instant messaging   camera phones   microwave ovens   (your own idea)

1. What is your opinion about this technology?

   The computer technoloy was developped. So. everything became
   very convenient and busy. So, we can   send

2. a. Now write a topic sentence for your paragraph: _message easily, quickly._

   we can required to send message easily, quickly.

   b. Circle the topic and underline the controlling idea.

D Make notes of ideas that you could use in your paragraph to explain this topic sentence. (You do NOT need complete sentences.)

_____   _____

_____   _____

_____   _____

_____   _____

E Now choose the best ideas from D, and write your paragraph.

1 VOCABULARY & EXPRESSIONS

A Complete the sentences with an expression from the box. Add articles (*a/an*) where needed.

> early riser   heartbreaker   night owl   hothead
> home body   free spirit   risk taker   team player

1. Dave is definitely _____. He'll try anything, and he never worries about making mistakes.

2. We need _____ for this project, someone who can work closely with the other software designers.

3. I wish my boyfriend weren't such _____. He gets angry and yells a lot just about every time he drives.

4. My roommate is really _____. Yesterday he started cooking dinner at midnight!

5. Since last year, I've become _____. I go to the gym at 6 A.M. most days and work out for an hour.

6. It seems like Gina has a new boyfriend every month. She must be a real _____.

7. Don't be such _____! You need to go out and have fun more often. Let's go dancing!

8. When I was younger, I was really _____. I did whatever I wanted, and I never thought about the future.

B What personality characteristics are important for these people? Use vocabulary from the unit and other words you know.

A good friend	A good employee	A good teacher	A good parent

C Answer the questions using expressions from the box.

> In general   For the most part   Typically   As a rule   Normally

1. When do you do your English homework?

   _____

2. What kind of food do you like?

   _____

3. What do you do after dinner?

   _____

4. Where do you like to go with your friends?

   _____

A Choose the correct word.

1. I didn't go to class yesterday _____ I had a doctor's appointment then.
   a. because   b. whenever   c. although

2. I take my dog for a walk in the park _____ the weather is nice.
   a. though   b. so that   c. whenever

3. _____ Jeff knew about the test for a month, he didn't study for it until the night before.
   a. Since   b. Although   c. So that

4. _____ my sister is a real hothead. She's always in trouble with her boss.
   a. Since   b. Even though   c. So that

5. I put my books next to the door _____ I wouldn't forget to take them back to the library.
   a. since   b. so that   c. though

6. _____ my friends invite me to parties almost every weekend, I just stay home and relax.
   a. Since   b. Whenever   c. Although

7. I've been going to the gym every day _____ I want to get in shape before summer.
   a. so that   b. because   c. whenever

8. _____ I'm a night owl, I get up before 6:00 on work days.
   a. Because   b. Even though   c. When

B Match the clauses and write each sentence two ways, using commas where needed.

Example: I'll send him an e-mail/when I have time
I'll send him an e-mail when I have time. / When I have time, I'll send him an e-mail.

1. I get really nervous	a. because it was raining
2. Jesse plays tennis outside all year	b. since we arrived late at night
3. we went right to our hotel	c. although it's hot here in summer
4. the soccer game was cancelled	d. whenever I have to go to the dentist

1. _____
   _____

2. _____
   _____

3. _____
   _____

4. _____
   _____

C Write true sentences using your own ideas.

1. Although _____, I _____.

2. Since _____, I _____.

3. I _____ when I _____.

4. I _____ even though I _____.

5. I usually _____ because _____.

6. I _____ so that _____.

7. Whenever I _____, I _____.

Personality

| *Lesson B* | What type are you? |

1 READING

A Read this description of a system for studying people's personalities.

The Enneagram

Some psychologists use a system called the *enneagram* to study people's personalities. The word *enneagram* comes from the Greek words for *nine* and *picture,* and the system describes nine different types of people. Which number are you?

Number 1: _____ These people try for excellence in everything they do. They worry a lot about making mistakes, and always want to be "the best." They sometimes criticize other people who don't try hard enough. Often, they feel there is only one right way of thinking and doing things, but they can be **playful** when they are on vacation or away from their usual tasks.

Number 2: _____ These people are warm, concerned, nurturing, and sensitive. They are happiest when they are helping other people, and friendships are very important to them. At times, they forget about their own needs. They are flexible and can adapt their personality to give different people what they want. This type finds it easy to be a pushover, and very difficult to be independent.

Number 3: _____ These people are go-getters—energetic, optimistic, motivated, and productive. They are very concerned with results and success, and can become overachievers and workaholics, with no time for emotions. Their biggest fear is failure, and they are happiest when other people see their accomplishments.

Number 4: _____ These people love to experience intense emotion and have very sensitive feelings. Emotional honesty is very important, and they are always looking for someone who will make them feel special. They are very creative, and often, they find their daily routine ordinary and boring—they like to have **drama** in their lives.

Number 5: _____ These introverted, **curious** people have a strong need for knowledge and love to study and analyze. Many of them don't feel comfortable interacting with other people—they prefer to be alone and removed from the world. They have a difficult time with feelings, and instead, they try to gain more understanding of the world.

Number 6: _____ These people are responsible, trustworthy, and always **loyal** to their family, their friends, and the things they believe in. It's important for them to belong to a group that accepts them. They tend to worry a lot. Some are reserved and shy, others are outgoing and even aggressive, but all of them have a great need to feel safe and secure.

Number 7: _____ These people are always looking for new and exciting experiences, and are optimistic about the future. They want to make the world a better place. They don't like rules and restrictions, and they enjoy change because they get bored easily. They are **sociable** and outgoing, and always try to find enjoyment in life.

Number 8: _____ These people are direct and self-reliant. They want to make all of their own decisions. Independence is very important to them, and they like to have power and authority over other people. They are very self-confident and assertive. They are protective of their family and friends, and they often rebel against authority.

Number 9: _____ These people want to bring **harmony** to other people and to the world around them. In any situation, they will try to help people understand each other. They are sincere, patient, and easy-going. Often, they have too many things to do because it's difficult for them to say "No." They have a talent for seeing all sides of an issue.

B Write the names of the types in the correct section of the reading.

> The Scientist   The Team Member   The Adventurer   The Independent   The Peacemaker
> The Perfectionist   The Helper   The Achiever   The Romantic

C Look at the words from the reading in bold. Choose the correct answer by thinking about the context of the word.

1. Sociable is similar in meaning to _____.
   a. outgoing   b. introverted   c. driven

2. A playful person doesn't feel _____.
   a. driven   b. relaxed   c. happy

3. If you are loyal to your family, you always _____ them.
   a. criticize   b. avoid   c. support

4. Harmony is similar to _____.
   a. agreement   b. arguing   c. asking questions

5. A curious person wants to _____ a lot of new things.
   a. buy   b. learn about   c. avoid

6. In this context, drama means _____.
   a. stories   b. acting   c. excitement

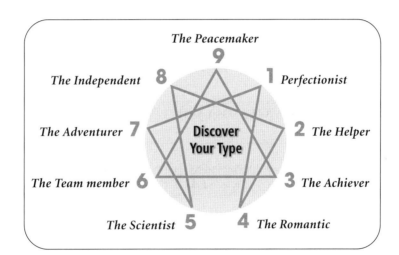

D Answer the questions.

1. Which type from the reading do you think you are? _____

2. Why does this description fit you? _____

   _____

3. Which of these types would be easy for you to get along with? _____

   Why? _____

   _____

4. Which of these types would be hard for you to get along with? _____

   Why? _____

   _____

> The topic sentence states the main idea in a paragraph. Every sentence in the paragraph must be related to the topic sentence.

A Each of these paragraphs contains one sentence that doesn't fit with the topic sentence. Find it and cross it out.

1. There are a number of reasons why I decided to study engineering. I always enjoyed my math and science courses when I was in high school. My university is one of the largest in my country. Engineers can work in many important fields, such as alternative energy and pollution control. Also, my country needs many more engineers for its future development. For all these reasons, I chose electrical engineering as my major.

2. Running is one of the healthiest forms of exercise. It strengthens all of the muscles in your lower body, and increases coordination. It improves the functioning of your heart and lungs. Because it burns a large number of calories, it can help you to control your weight. Every year, many runners have foot problems because they don't wear the right shoes. Furthermore, studies have found that runners get fewer colds and other illnesses than non-runners.

3. I've known my friend Kaitlyn for a long time. We met on the first day of high school, and we've seen each other almost every day since then. Her parents are divorced. She's easygoing and optimistic, and a lot of fun to be with. We often go out dancing or go to parties together. I'm kind of a hothead, but Kaitlyn always calms me down and gives me good advice when I'm upset. I'm lucky to have a friend like Kaitlyn.

4. One of the most important food plants in the world today is rice. Nearly half of the world's population eats rice every day of their lives. In certain Asian countries, the average person consumes 100 to 200 kg of rice per year. Fried rice is a delicious dish that's not difficult to cook. In some languages, people don't greet each other with "How are you?", but "Have you eaten rice today?"

> A **descriptive paragraph** tells what something or someone is like. It should contain specific details that help your reader understand your subject.

B Look at the picture and write new sentences that include specific details. Use information from the picture, and your imagination.

1. Jessica is pretty.

   She has long, curly dark hair and big dark eyes.

2. She's serious.

   _____

   _____

3. She likes music.

   _____

   _____

4. She's ambitious.

   _____

   _____

5. She likes animals.

   _____

   _____

6. (your own idea)

   _____

   _____

C You are going to write a descriptive paragraph about a person who is important in your life—now, or in the past. First, make notes to help you write. Think of specific details.

Appearance:

_____   _____

_____   _____

_____   _____

Personality:

_____   _____

_____   _____

_____   _____

Behavior:

_____   _____

_____   _____

_____   _____

D Now write your paragraph, using the correct format.

Make an Impact

Lesson A | Change your world

1 VOCABULARY & EXPRESSIONS

A Complete the sentences with the correct form of a word from the box. Add articles if needed.

> generation   escapist   activist   motivated
> issue   visionary   tradition   apathetic

1. _____ is someone who doesn't like to think about the real world and its problems.

2. Environmental _____ in our country are working to save the rainforests from destruction.

3. My brother is completely _____ about world events. He doesn't even read the newspaper.

4. One of the most controversial _____ in my country is whether to build a dam across our largest river.

5. Nobel Peace Prize winners are _____ who have wonderful ideas to bring peace to the world.

6. Many young people today are very _____ and are working hard for international understanding.

7. In my country we have _____ of providing a good education for even the poorest children.

8. Many people of the older _____ aren't really interested in computers and technology.

B Answer the questions with your own ideas.

1. Who is an important activist in your country? What has this person done? _____

   _____

2. What generation do you belong to? _____

   _____

3. What are some issues in your country or in the world that are important to you? Why? _____

   _____

C Match the parts of the expressions for agreeing and disagreeing.

1. I'm not _____   a. think so.
2. You may be right _____   b. come on!
3. That seems _____   c. point, but...
4. I hate to _____   d. something there.
5. You may have _____   e. disagree with you, but . . .
6. Oh, _____   f. so sure about that.
7. I know _____   g. I agree with you.
8. I'm not sure that _____ h. about that.
9. I see your _____   i. what you mean, but . . .
10. I don't _____   j. a little bit extreme.

A Match sentences 1–10 with descriptions of the situations a–j.

1. I brought my umbrella with me, but I didn't have to use it. _____

2. Students are allowed to borrow up to ten books from the library each week. _____

3. I think you should stop drinking soda if you want to lose weight. _____

4. I was able to swim before I was six years old because my father taught me. _____

5. Dolores can run 10 km in less than an hour. _____

6. We are required to write a book report every week for our literature class. _____

7. You don't have to answer that question if you don't want to. _____

8. Jason had to work until midnight every night last week. _____

9. When I was ten years old, I was permitted to take the bus downtown by myself. _____

10. You should have listened to your friends and applied for that job. _____

a. advice (present)
b. advice (past)
c. permission (present)
d. permission (past)
e. necessity (present)
f. necessity (past)
g. lack of necessity (present)
h. lack of necessity (past)
i. ability (present)
j. ability (past)

B Correct one mistake in each sentence.

1. I was able to found all the information that I needed on a website.

2. We could to use our dictionaries during the English exam.

3. Nick should have go to Europe when he had the chance last year.

4. People aren't required to bring big suitcases with them onto the airplane.

5. Were you have to cook all the food for the party by yourself?

6. You can get a driver's license if you want to drive anywhere in this country.

C Complete the sentences with your own ideas.

1. In this class, we aren't required to _____.

2. Children shouldn't be permitted to _____.

3. When I was ten years old, I was able to _____.

4. I think teenagers should be allowed to _____.

5. If you want to speak English well, you have to _____.

6. To enroll in this school, students are required to _____.

Make an Impact

Lesson B | Take a stand

1 READING

A Read this web page.

My Trash, Your Treasure

In 2003, Deron Beal faced an unusual problem. In his work as an activist for a recycling group in Tucson, Arizona, he had collected a lot of used couches, computers, office chairs, and desks that businesses no longer needed. What could he do with them? He didn't want to send them to a landfill. So he sent out an e-mail to all the non-profit organizations he knew nearby, asking if they could use some office furniture. Within days, all the furniture had gone to people and groups who could use it.

That was the beginning of Freecycle, an online system that lets people give away things they no longer want, instead of putting them in the garbage. Today, more than a million people participate in 2,417 groups around the world. There are 166 members in the Budapest group, 77 in Hong Kong, and 102 in Sao Paulo. New groups are forming every day.

The Freecycling process is simple. You begin by joining your local Freecycle e-mail group. If you have a chair that you don't want, you post a message with the subject "Offered: Chair." If you're looking for a chair, you post a message with the heading "Wanted: Chair." If you see a possible match, you e-mail the person and make arrangements to get the item. The only rule is that everything must be free, with no payment or exchanges.

Baby clothes, old magazines, cans of paint, old sewing machines, used computers and cell phones—people offer an endless variety of things on Freecycle. The same is true for the kinds of things people hunt for online. You'll find requests for old cookbooks, golf shoes—even goldfish.

In some places, Freecycle groups have worked to help people who have lost everything in their homes in a fire. In Canada, a woman who volunteers by planting gardens in schools gets all of her flowers from Freecycle. One Freecycle member donated her old wedding dress to a woman who couldn't afford one.

According to the group's website, the worldwide Freecycle Network is made up of many individual groups across the globe. It's a grassroots movement of people who want to give (and get) stuff for free in their own towns. Each group is run by a local volunteer, and membership is free. To sign up, people visit **www.freecycle.org** and then click the link for the group nearest them. If there isn't a group nearby, the website gives instructions for starting a new local group.

Freecycle's motto is "Changing the world, one gift at a time." Deron Beal's visionary idea is a gift to us all.

B Choose the correct answer.

1. Freecycle is a kind of _____.
   a. store   b. online service   c. magazine

2. People who list things on Freecycle want to _____.
   a. give them away   b. sell them   c. buy them

3. To use Freecycle, you must first _____.
   a. join a group near you   b. buy a membership   c. both *a* and *b*

4. If you want to get something from Freecycle, you have to _____.
   a. send an order   b. call Freecycle   c. write an e-mail

5. The purpose of Freecycle is to _____.
   a. help people find things   b. keep things out of the garbage   c. both *a* and *b*

C Find the underlined words in the reading with these meanings.

1. started by ordinary people _____

2. a place where garbage is buried in the ground _____

3. gave to help someone _____

4. take part in _____

5. charity _____

D List three examples of each of these things.

1. items that Deron Beal had collected _____

   _____

2. cities where there are Freecycle groups _____

   _____

3. things that people have offered _____

   _____

4. things that people have asked for _____

   _____

5. people who have received help from Freecycle _____

   _____

E Answer the questions.

1. Do you think Freecycle would work in your country? Why or why not?

   _____

   _____

2. What do you usually do with old things that you don't use any more? Why?

   _____

   _____

A Write a topic sentence for each of these paragraphs. Be sure to include a controlling idea that tells the writer's attitude towards the topic.

1. _____
   _____

My room in the dormitory is very small, and I have to share it with two other students. One of my roommates stays up very late at night studying and the other listens to the radio all the time. It's difficult to study in there, or even to sleep. The food in the cafeteria isn't very good, and it seems like we have chicken almost every day. I really hope to get my own apartment next year.

2. _____
   _____

More than 300 million people speak English as their first language, and millions of others have learned it in school. In countries such as India and Pakistan, people with different native languages use it as a means of communication. English is the common language in a number of industries, from aviation to software, and it's also a useful language for travel nearly anywhere in the world. For all of these reasons, more and more people around the world are enrolling in English classes.

3. _____
   _____

Hawaii's climate is sunny and pleasant all year, and temperatures are never extremely hot or cold. Every island has lovely beaches and spectacular tropical scenery. Facilities for tourists are excellent, with hotels in all price ranges and a wide variety of restaurants. And there are direct flights to Hawaii from countries all around the world. All of these factors have helped Hawaii attract growing numbers of visitors.

4. _____
   _____

For one thing, dogs are very intelligent. I've had a lot of fun teaching my dog tricks, and he knows ten different words now. Besides that, dogs are useful. My dog keeps my house safe—he makes so much noise that no thief will ever try to get in. Finally, dogs are great companions. My dog loves to go everywhere with me, and I take him along on rides in my car, hikes, and even swimming at the beach. A good dog can be your best friend.

Newspapers around the world print letters to the editor from their readers. These letters must be short, and should give reasons to explain the opinion.

B Look at this letter to the editor and label these parts with words from the box. Notice how they are arranged.

(address   body   closing   date   greeting   signature)

1. ☐

418 Center Avenue
Metropolis City 02210
December 12, 2005

3. ☐

2. ☐

Dear Editor:

Smoking is one of the biggest threats to our health, but we aren't doing enough to protect non-smokers. In offices and other workplaces, employees are forced to breathe pollution from colleagues who smoke. It's difficult to find a restaurant where diners can escape from other people's cigarettes. On an inter-city bus or train, you might be forced to inhale dangerous smoke for up to ten hours. We need laws to make all our public places smoke-free.

4. ☐

5. ☐

Sincerely,
Hassan Ali

6. ☐

C You are going to write a letter to the editor. Choose one of these topics:

(garbage   traffic   noise   (your own idea))

Write a topic sentence with a controlling idea that states your opinion about this topic.

_____

Think of three reasons for your opinion that you can use in supporting sentences.

1. _____

2. _____

3. _____

D Now write your letter, following the letter format in B. Be sure to explain your reasons.

_____
_____
_____
_____
_____
_____
_____
_____
_____
_____
_____
_____

1 VOCABULARY & EXPRESSIONS

A Complete the police reports with words from the box. Use each word only once.

sought	devoted	stranded	distress call	authorities
involvement	seemingly	vanished	outcome	identified
documents	evidence	theory	incident	witness

Police Reports

(1) _____ are searching for a dangerous prisoner who escaped from City Jail. Buster Jones (2) _____ from his cell some time late last night. Guards at the prison have a (3) _____ that other prisoners helped him by turning off the prison's alarm system. A (4) _____ said that he saw Jones in the hall, but didn't think anything of it.

Police arrested Maybelle Maples, age 72, for stealing over $2 million from the bank where she worked for 50 years. Her employers found a folder of (5) _____ that showed she had taken the money from customers' accounts. Her colleagues said Maples was a (6) _____ employee, who always worked hard at the bank and stayed late every night. "I can't believe that a (7) _____ helpful old woman could do such a thing," said one coworker. "But, they (8) _____ her handwriting on those papers, so it must be true."

Highway patrol officers helped a man whose car went off the road on the way to his own wedding. They received a (9) _____ on a cell phone from Keith Sanders, who was (10) _____ at the side of the highway. "I guess I wasn't thinking about my driving," said Sanders. "But I got to my wedding on time. I'm so grateful for this happy (11) _____."

A local woman is being (12) _____ for stealing valuable jewelry from several stores. There is (13) _____ that she may have had help from store employees, and they are being questioned about their (14) _____ in the thefts. Anyone with information about this (15) _____ is asked to contact the police.

B Rank these expressions in order from most certain (1) to least certain (6).

a. _____ I'm pretty sure that

b. _____ I'm positive that

c. _____ I know that

d. _____ I suppose that

e. _____ I wonder if

f. _____ I suspect that

A What happened? For each situation, use three different modal expressions from the box to make guesses.

> must (not) have   might (not) have   may (not) have   could (not) have

A.

1. She _____
   _____
2. _____
   _____
3. _____
   _____

B.

4. Their friends _____
   _____
5. _____
   _____
6. _____
   _____

C.

7. _____
   _____
8. _____
9. _____
   _____

D.

10. _____
    _____
11. _____
    _____
12. _____
    _____

B Rewrite these sentences using a modal expression of speculation.

1. It's not possible that you wrote this paper yourself.

   _____

2. We can conclude that Jim Thompson didn't plan his disappearance.

   _____

3. It's certain that Jim Thompson wanted to vanish.

   _____

4. Maybe our teacher forgot about our quiz today.

   _____

Believe It or Not

Lesson B | More mysteries

A Read this article about a mysterious place in Peru.

Earth's Most Mysterious Places:

Nazca

In a remote area of Peru, 300 kilometers from Lima, one of the most unusual works of art in the world has baffled scientists for decades. Seen from the ground, it looks like nothing at all: just lines scratched into the earth. But from high above, it is clear that these marks are something far more unusual. Huge images of birds, fish, seashells, and geometric shapes are skillfully carved into the earth.

The geoglyphs of Nazca (the term comes from the Greek words for "earth picture") have been perfectly preserved for centuries by the desert's dry climate. The Nazca Lines are so difficult to see from the ground that they weren't discovered until the 1930s, when aircraft discovered them while flying over the area. In all, there are about 70 different human and animal figures on the plain, and almost 900 geometric shapes, including triangles, circles, and lines. They cover an area more than 60 kilometers long.

But who created these amazing shapes—and why? Researchers have determined that the geoglyphs are at least 1500 years old, but their purpose remains a mystery. Numerous theories have been offered. A Swiss writer named Erich von Daniken wrote that the Nazca Lines were designed as a landing place for travelers from other planets. However, it would probably be very confusing to try to land a spaceship in the middle of pictures of dogs, monkeys, and giant lizards.

In the 1940s, an American explorer named Paul Kosok suggested that the drawings were records of the movement of the stars and planets. He called Nazca "the largest astronomy book in the world." Later, an astronomer tested his theory by inputting information about the lines and different astronomical events into a computer. The computer could find no relationship between the two.

Another explanation is that the lines may have been made for religious reasons. British researcher Tony Morrison investigated the customs of people in the Andes Mountains, and learned that they have a long tradition of praying at shrines by the side of the road. Some of their shrines are just simple piles of stones. It's possible that in the past, the lines of Nazca were created for a similar purpose, on a much larger scale. The largest pictures may have been the sites for special ceremonies.

Recently, two other scientists, David Johnson and Steve Mabee, have speculated that the geoglyphs could have been related to water. Nazca is one of the driest places in the world, and receives only two centimeters of rain every year. While Johnson was searching for ancient water sources in the area, he noticed that some waterways built by ancient people were connected with the lines. Johnson believes that the Nazca lines are a giant map of the underground water in the area. Other scientists are now looking for evidence to confirm this theory.

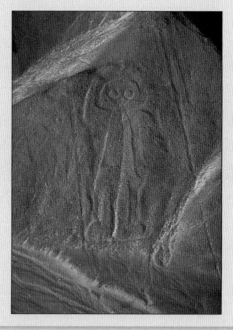

B Complete the chart with information from the reading.

	1.	2.	3.	4.
Name				
Nationality		American		
Theory			People used them to pray as they walked along the road.	
Evidence FOR or AGAINST this theory	This would not be a good way to land a spaceship.			Ancient waterways were connected with the lines.

C Answer the questions.

1. Which of these theories seems the most reasonable to you? Why?

_____

_____

_____

2. Scientists don't know how the Nazca art was made without using aerial equipment. How do you think they did it? Make up two theories of your own.

a. _____

_____

b. _____

_____

3. What do you think future archeologists will find from our time that seems mysterious?

_____

_____

When you write a summary, you give all the most important points from a reading in your own words. You must not copy sentences directly from the passage.

A Read this article about a mysterious island.

The Mystery of Easter Island, by Javier Perez

Over time, developments in archeology and exploration have led to many new discoveries about ancient cultures and how they lived. However, there are still some places on earth that still hold mysteries for scientists, and some of them are the subject of much discussion and speculation. One of the most mysterious is Easter Island.

Located in the South Pacific, Easter Island is one of the most remote places on earth, and it is best known for the enormous stone statues that stand along its coast. These statues were carved by ancient people to resemble human heads, and are between 3 and 13 meters in height. More than 600 of these statues remain.

Archeological research has determined that the statues are around 1500 years old, and were made by the island's first inhabitants, people who came from the islands in the western Pacific. Scientists believe that the enormous heads were carved from volcanic rock, and then pulled to their different locations. The statues may have been carved for religious reasons.

We may never know the true reason behind the carving of the Easter Island statues. But whatever their original purpose, they are a wonderful example of human skill and creativity.

B Now answer these questions in complete sentences, and write the answers in paragraph format. This will give you a summary.

1. Why is Easter Island famous?

2. What do the Easter Island statues look like, and how big are they?

3. What do scientists know about the statues?

4. What aren't they sure about?

5. Why are the statues important?

An article by Javier Perez describes the "mystery of Easter Island." _____

_____

_____

_____

_____

_____

_____

C Read the following article and write a short summary.

The Ruins of Stonehenge, by Chris Greaves

Stonehenge is one of the most popular tourist attractions in Europe—as well as the most mysterious. At this ancient site in southern England, a collection of large stones is arranged in two large circles, one inside the other. Although only ruins of the inner circle exist today, scientists believe it was built first. The giant stones of the outer circle weigh as much as 5,000 kg each!

Exactly why Stonehenge was built remains a mystery. Research suggests that it may have been built by an ancient religious group who used it as an observatory to study the movements of the stars and planets. Some experts disagree, saying that it was built as a temple.

In any case, the construction of Stonehenge was an amazing achievement. There are no building stones in that area of England, so the stones might have been transported from up to 400 km away to their present site. Engineers have calculated that about 600 people must have worked together to move each of the giant stones to its location.

Today, thousands of tourists come every year to marvel at Stonehenge. It's difficult to believe that these remarkable structures were built without modern machinery.

Today's Workplace

| *Lesson A* | Work issues |

1 VOCABULARY & EXPRESSIONS

A Rewrite these sentences using a phrasal verb from the box. Use the correct form.

| find out | give up | go under | set up |
| cut back on | lay off | figure out | take off |

1. My doctor says I need to reduce the amount of sugar that I eat every day.

   _____

2. The factory sent home a lot of their workers last month because production was down.

   _____

3. At the city council meeting, we learned about the plan to build a museum.

   _____

4. Sales of our new chocolate drink have really increased in the last two months.

   _____

5. Our soccer team didn't win any games this year, but we're not going to stop trying.

   _____

6. Sandy is trying to solve the problem of whether she should look for a new job.

   _____

7. Last year Jason established his own website design business.

   _____

8. I was afraid my company might fail, but this year it's doing much better.

   _____

B Complete the conversation with expressions from the box.

| that will be fine | that's not possible | would you consider |
| I'm afraid I can't | bear in mind that | if you'll . . . I could |

Leslie: Professor Scott, could I possibly take the final exam a week later? My brother is getting married on the day of the exam.

Prof. Scott: No, I'm sorry, (1) _____. I need to submit my students' grades the day after the exam.

Leslie: In that case, (2) _____ letting me take the exam early?

Prof. Scott: (3) _____ do that. I would have to write a different exam for the rest of the class.

Leslie: Well, please (4) _____ you said our term paper was more important that the exam . . . What about if I wrote an extra term paper?

Prof. Scott: Hmm . . . (5) _____ write two papers, _____ excuse you from taking the exam.

Leslie: (6) _____. Thanks, professor.

2 GRAMMAR

A Complete the phrasal verbs with the appropriate phrase from the box. If the phrasal verb doesn't take an object, write *intransitive*.

Mr. Lu for a promotion
a plan for increasing sales
my assignment to the teacher

the money we spend on entertainment
the meeting until next month

an interesting new invention
buying a new car

1. carry out _____

2. get ahead _____

3. hang on _____

4. hand in _____

5. pass over _____

6. put off _____

7. catch on _____

8. come up with _____

9. think about _____

10. go under _____

11. give up _____

12. cut back on _____

B Correct one mistake in each sentence.

1. Jenna's company designs and set ups new computer systems for schools.

2. You have to work really hard if you want to get a head, and you can't give up.

3. I was very upset when I find out that my husband was laid off from his job.

4. We're trying to come off with some new ideas for advertising our organic coffee.

C What is the boss saying to his employees? Write sentences using phrasal verbs from the unit.

1. _____

2. _____

3. _____

4. _____

5. _____

Today's Workplace

| *Lesson B* | Job choices |

A Read this article about four successful people.

TODAY Magazine talks to . . .

People Who Love Their Work

Denise Barrett, movie critic

"When I was a little kid, I loved to go to the movies every Saturday—and now my newspaper pays me to see them! Sometimes I have to <u>take in</u> three or four in one day, but it's still fun. Then I go back to my home office, write my reviews, and e-mail them to my editor. What I enjoy the most is writing about great new films by young directors—I think I can help their careers by attracting a bigger audience for their films. Of course, there are some drawbacks to this work. Sometimes readers send angry letters if I write a negative review about a movie they enjoyed. But I can understand that, because I have strong opinions myself."

Marisol Castro, food photographer

"You know those beautiful photos in cookbooks? Well, that's what I do all day— shoot photographs of food! I used to be a chef, but I got tired of preparing the same dishes night after night. So I <u>branched out</u> into writing cookbooks, and then into photography. I've worked all around the world, and I never do the same thing two days in a row. Typically, I take dozens and dozens of pictures! But I never get bored. The only thing I don't like about my job is carrying heavy bags—ingredients and equipment. But I need the exercise, because of course I have to <u>check out</u> the food after I photograph it!"

Elizabeth Crowden, wedding dress designer

"I design and make custom wedding dresses for the bride and sometimes for the other women in the ceremony. I just love working for such a happy occasion! Of course there's a lot of pressure, because everything has to be ready on time, and there are so many details to <u>work out.</u> But I just love to see the bride's face when she <u>tries on</u> her wedding dress for the first time. Of course I take pictures—would you like to see some? You know, every time I make a dress, I feel like I'm getting married all over again. It's a really joyful job."

Michael Tani, surfing school owner

"The best thing about my job is that now I get to be out in the sun and the waves every day. No more office or commuting for me! I give lessons to both men and women, and here in Hawaii, the season is all year round. People sometimes ask me what it's like being on vacation all the time—they don't understand that this really is work. Some students <u>pick up</u> surfing very quickly, but others need a lot more patience and encouragement. But it's wonderful to see them stand up on the surfboard and ride their first wave!"

B Check the correct answers.

Who . . .	Denise	Marisol	Elizabeth	Angela
1. uses a camera at work?	☐	☐	☐	☐
2. travels for her job?	☐	☐	☐	☐
3. works outdoors?	☐	☐	☐	☐
4. has a strict schedule?	☐	☐	☐	☐
5. is a teacher?	☐	☐	☐	☐
6. has an office?	☐	☐	☐	☐
7. works only with women?	☐	☐	☐	☐
8. uses a computer?	☐	☐	☐	☐
9. had a different job in the past?	☐	☐	☐	☐

C What is the negative point of each dream job? Answer in your own words.

1. movie critic _____

_____

2. food photographer _____

_____

3. wedding dress designer _____

_____

4. surfing school owner _____

_____

D Match the phrasal verbs from the reading with their meanings.

1. take in		a. learn
2. branch out		b. investigate, test
3. check out		c. plan, solve
4. work out		d. go to see
5. try on		e. put on for the first time
6. pick up		f. try something different

A Rewrite these parts of a business letter in the correct format.

a. I would like to receive information about your summer internship program. I am a student at National University majoring in business administration. I am interested in getting experience in international business before I graduate next year. Thank you for your assistance.

b. Andrew Kwan

c. 632 Rosewood Lane
   Capital City 53216

d. Sincerely yours,

e. Ms. Annette Deane
   Global Exports Ltd.
   2300 Global Drive
   Capital City 53207

f. February 12, 2005

g. Dear Ms. Deane:

h. Andrew Kwan

B Match the parts of the letter with their names.

Body _____

Return address _____

Date _____

Closing _____

Inside address _____

Greeting _____

Signature _____

C Read this advertisement and write a letter to say that you're interested in this program. Use business letter format.

Try out Your Dream Job!

Have you always wanted to be a flight attendant? a rock musician? a fashion model?

We're looking for people to appear on our new reality TV show, "Dream Job." You'll spend a week working at your dream job along with a professional—and seeing what it's like in reality. For more information, write to us and tell us a little bit about yourself, and your dream job. You could be one of the five lucky people who will appear in next season's hottest new show!

Contact: Alan Dunham, Metro TV, P.O. Box 8210, Capital City 53713

Language Summaries

Unit 1 *What's the Story?*

Lesson A

Vocabulary Focus

alter
cover
go after
go over
interpret
make up
piece together
verify

Additional Vocabulary

change a / one's story
kill a story

Language Focus

Review of the simple past and present perfect

Speaking:

Telling stories

I'll never forget the time . . .
Did I ever tell you about the time . . .
A couple of years ago . . .
Last summer . . .
It happened when . . .
One night . . .
All of a sudden . . .
Suddenly . . .
What happened in the end was . . .
In the end . . .
Looking back on it, . . .
It seems funny now, but . . .

Listening to stories

Wow!
Really!
Are you kidding?
Are you joking?
Unbelievable!

And then what happened?
What did you do next?
Do you mean?
Did you say?

Lesson B

Vocabulary

consequences
expectantly
family
fate
magic charm
solemnly
sorry
stormy night
visitor
wish
your loss

Unit 2 *Technology*

Lesson A

Vocabulary Focus

dependence
impersonal
information overload
interaction
liberating
multitask
promote
recipe for disaster
sedentary

Additional Vocabulary

cure for
dealings with
dependence on
get to the bottom of
  (something)

Language Focus

Review of the passive voice

Speaking:

Saying you're able/not able to do something

I might be able to . . .
I'm pretty good at . . .
I haven't got a clue about . . .
I know something about . . .
I'm no good at . . .
I don't have the faintest idea.

Lesson B

Vocabulary

anonymously
at stake
automatically
benefit
device
display
embed
privacy
track
unique

Unit 3 *Personality*

Lesson A

Vocabulary Focus

control freak   overachiever
early riser   pushover
go-getter   risk taker
hothead   self-starter

Additional Vocabulary

even though
free spirit
heartbreaker
homebody
night owl
team player

Language Focus

Adverb clauses of contrast, purpose, and time

Speaking:
Making general statements

Generally speaking . . .
In general . . .
For the most part . . .
Typically . . .
As a rule . . .
Normally . . .

Lesson B

Vocabulary

assertive
driven
easygoing
introspective
let someone go
nurturing
optimistic
peaceful
refined
systematic
unpredictable

Unit 4 *Make an Impact*

Lesson A

Vocabulary Focus

activists
apathetic
aware
carry on this tradition
circumstances
escapist
generation
issues
motivated
visionary

Additional Vocabulary

amoral
apolitical
asocial
atypical
internship
slacker

Language Focus

Modals and phrasal modals

Speaking:
Exchanging ideas in a non-confrontational way

Exactly!
Definitely!
I completely agree.
You may be right about . . .
You're absolutely right!
You may have something there.

I hate to disagree with you, but . . .
I see your point, but . . .
I know what you mean, but . . .
You may be right in part, but . . .

Yeah, but I don't think so.
I'm not so sure about that.
I'm not sure I agree with you.

That seems a bit extreme.
Oh, come on!
No way!

Lesson B

Vocabulary

business as usual
do your part
hack into
promote
public service announcements
raise awareness
solution
speak out against
think outside the box

Language Summaries

Unit 5 *Believe It or Not*

Lesson A

Vocabulary Focus

authority	outcome
devoted	seemingly
distress call	vanished
document	sought
evidence	strand
identify	theory
incident	witness
involvement	

Additional Vocabulary

adopt	premises
can't tell two	run into
people apart	to say the least
have a lot	twist of fate
in common	whereabouts
only child	
out of the ordinary	
outskirts	

Language Focus

Modals of speculation about the past

Speaking:
Making speculations

I wonder if . . .
I suppose . . .
I suspect that . . .
I'm pretty sure that . . .
I'm convinced/certain/positive that . . .
It's impossible that . . .
There's no doubt that . . .

Responding to speculations

Definitely!
You're probably right.
You may be right.
Well, maybe, but . . .
That hardly seems likely.
No way! (informal)

Lesson B

Vocabulary

inexplicable
intuition
malfunction
observe
previous
routinely
speculate
trigger

Unit 6 *Today's Workplace*

Lesson A

Vocabulary Focus

catch on	go under
come up with	hand in
cut back on	lay off
figure out	pass over
find out	set up
get ahead	stick with
give up	take off

Additional Vocabulary

get away
get back to
get by
get into
goof off
got behind

Language Focus

Phrasal verbs

Speaking:
Negotiating a solution

Would you consider . . . if I . . .
If you'll . . . I could . . .
Bear in mind . . .
Remember that . . .
I can agree to that.
That will be fine.
That's not possible.
I'm afraid I can't.

Lesson B

Vocabulary

an opportunity in disguise
come around
have butterflies in (one's) stomach
so to speak

Grammar Summaries

Unit 1 *What's the Story?*

Language Focus: Review of the simple past and present perfect

Use the simple past to talk about actions that began and ended in the past. Use the present perfect for actions that began in the past and continue in the present:

My father **was** a reporter for thirty years. (He's retired now.)
My mother **has been** a reporter for thirty years. For the past 10 years, **she's worked** for *The Daily Standard.*
(She is still working as a reporter.)

If a specific time is mentioned in the past, use the simple past. If the time when something happened isn't mentioned, use the present perfect:

Have you ever **been** to Asia?   Yes, I **visited** Japan and Korea last year.
                                         Yes, I**'ve visited** both Japan and Korea.

Use the present perfect for past actions that have a connection to a present result:

The test **hasn't started** yet. We're still waiting for the teacher to arrive.

The adverbs *already, just, never, still,* and *yet* are often used with the present perfect. Some adverbs can also be used with the simple past with no change in meaning:

I've *never* **been** there, but I'd like to visit.
Bill *still* **hasn't phoned.** I hope he's OK.
Have you finished your homework *yet?* = Did you finish your homework yet?
Let me introduce Mia.   That's OK, we**'ve** *already* **met.** = That's OK, we already **met.**
Their plane **has** *just* **landed.** = Their plane just **landed.**

Unit 2 *Technology*

Language Focus: Review of the passive voice

Tense	Active Voice	Passive Voice
present	People in Morocco *speak* Arabic and French.	Arabic and French **are spoken** in Morocco.
present continuous	They*'re building* a new library on campus.	A new library **is being built** on campus.
present perfect	The airlines *have canceled* all flights due to bad weather.	All flights **have been canceled** due to bad weather.
past	The police *arrested* twenty people at yesterday's demonstration.	Twenty people **were arrested** at yesterday's demonstration.
future with *will*	The embassy *will mail* your visa to you.	Your visa **will be mailed** to you.

In a passive sentence, the object of an active sentence becomes the subject:

       subject   object   subject   agent
ACTIVE: <u>Willem Kolff</u> **invented** <u>the first artificial heart</u>.   PASSIVE: <u>The first artificial heart</u> **was invented** by <u>Willem Kolff</u>.

The agent is not always used in passive sentences. It is omitted when the agent is unknown, obvious, or has been previously mentioned. Also, it can be omitted to avoid having to say it:

The mail **is delivered** at noon everyday.
Professor Hu told us about the final exam. The format of the exam **was explained** in detail.
The store **was robbed** last night. We don't know who did it.

You can use the agent, especially if it gives additional or surprising information:

Several of today's household appliances **were invented** in the early twentieth century <u>by women</u>.

Unit 3 *Personality*

Language Focus: Adverb clauses of purpose, contrast, and time

Adverb clauses are dependent clauses. (They cannot stand alone and need a main clause to complete the sentence's meaning.) Adverb clauses answer the questions *why, when, how,* or *where* something happened:

      main clause   adverb clause
    I left the party early <u>because</u> I wasn't feeling well.

When the adverb clause comes before the main clause, put a comma after it:
    Because I wasn't feeling well, I left the party early.

Adverb clauses that show a reason or purpose for doing something (with *because, since,* and *so that*) answer the question *why*:
    I can't go out tonight **because / since** I have a lot of homework. (= reason for doing something)
    I took the early bus **so (that)** I could get to class on time. (= purpose for doing something)

In conversation, an adverb clause with *because* can stand alone to emphasize the reason for doing something. *Since* cannot be used in this way:
    Why are you leaving?   **Because I'm tired.** [~~Since I'm tired.~~]

Adverb clauses of time (with *when* or *whenever*) answer the question *when.* Often, *when* and *whenever* both mean "every time that something happens." Use *when* if the meaning is "at the specific time that something happened":
    When(ever) I have to speak in front of the class, I get nervous.
    When Jamie called yesterday morning, I was sleeping. (~~Whenever Jamie called~~ . . .)

Adverb clauses of opposition or contrast (with *though, although,* and *even though*) are used to introduce a different or surprising idea. The words can be used with no change in meaning:
    Although / Even though / Though the cell phone was expensive, I bought it anyway.

Despite the fact (that) can also be used to introduce an adverb clause of contrast:
    Despite the fact that he lied to me, I still consider Darin to be my best friend.

Unit 4 *Make an Impact*

Language Focus: Modals and phrasal modals

Can and *be able to* are used to talk about ability. When speaking about something that took place in the past, use *could* to say someone was able to do something in general at any time. Use *was/were able to* to indicate someone managed to do something:
    Can you ski?
    She **could** read music by the time she was three.
    He **was able to** finish the race in under an hour. (~~He could finish the race . . .~~)

We can also talk about ability using *know how to*:
    Do you **know how to** speak Russian?

May and *can* are often used to give permission, but *can* is more informal:
    You **may** use your dictionaries to complete this exercise.
    You **can** stay as late as you'd like. Just don't forget to turn off the lights when you leave.

There is no past form of *may* for giving permission. Notice the past forms:
    You **may / You're allowed to** park here after 7 P.M.
    He said you **could / were allowed to** park here after 7 P.M.

Must expresses an obligation or sense of urgency. *Have to* is more commonly used to express necessity. (There is no past form of *must* for expressing necessity. Use *had to* instead.)

> It's not safe here. Everyone **must** leave the building immediately.
> At the lecture last night, I **had to** show my identification card to enter the building.

Should have is used to show regret about the past:

> I'm too busy to take a vacation. I **should've** gone to Hawaii when I had the chance.

Be supposed to can be used to talk about what you should or shouldn't do:

> What are you doing at home? **Aren't** you **supposed to** be at work today?
> You**'re not supposed to** use your cell phone here.

Unit 5 *Believe It or Not*

Language Focus: Modals of speculation about the past

We use *could have, might (not) have,* and *may (not) have* to make a guess about a situation in the past, based on partial information:

> The ancient tribes disappeared over 800 years ago. They **may have died** from starvation or
>   they **could have been killed** by disease. No one knows for sure.
> Ben **might not have gone** to bed yet. It looks like his bedroom light is still on.

Use *must have* when you are sure of your guess:

> The robbery **must have been** an inside job. There was no sign of forced entry.

Couldn't have and *can't have* indicate that the speaker thinks something is extremely unlikely or impossible:

> Bill **couldn't have driven** his car to work today. It's being repaired.

Unit 6 *Today's Workplace*

Language Focus: Phrasal verbs

Phrasal verbs are two-word and three-word verbs. They are made up of a verb + a particle. Some common particles are: *about, ahead, down, in, on, off, over, out, under,* and *up.*

When combined with a verb, the particle can change the meaning of the verb phrase:

> *give* = to offer something   *give up* = to quit doing something

Two-word transitive verbs (taking a direct object)		Two-word intransitive verbs (not taking a direct object)		Three-word verbs
carry out	put off	catch on	give up	come up with
cut back (on)	set up	get ahead	go under	get back to (someone)
figure out	stick with	get away	goof off	
hand in	think about	get behind	hang on	
lay off		get by	take off (*increase*)	
		get in		

Skills Index

Grammar

adopt/adapt, 63
Adverb clauses of contrast, purpose, and time, 28–29
Modals and phrasal modals, 42–43
Modals of speculation about the past, 54–55
Passive voice, 16–17
Phrasal verbs, 66–67
Prefixes, 31
Present perfect tense, 4
Simple past tense, 4
tell/say, 13

Listening

Interviews, 53, 65
Public service announcements, 49
Reports, 15
Skills
Asking and answering questions, 3, 4, 7, 8, 16, 17, 23, 27, 33, 34, 44, 45, 46, 53, 57, 59, 66, 69, 70, 73
Expressions showing listening, 6

Reading

Advertisements, 16, 45, 72
Articles, 60
Conversations, 30
Description, 32–33
Interviews, 69, 70–71
Letters, 57
News articles, 52–53
Paragraphs, 34
Statements, 64
Stories, 7, 8, 11, 54–55, 61
Skills
Distinguishing fact from theory, 58
Inferencing, 46–47, 70
Prereading activities, 7, 19–20, 31, 45, 57, 69
Skimming, 20–21, 58, 70–71

Speaking

Agreeing and disagreeing, 68
Asking and answering questions, 3, 4, 7, 8, 16, 17, 23, 27, 33, 34, 44, 45, 46, 53, 57, 59, 66, 69, 70, 73
Asking follow-up questions, 6
Cause and effect, 15
Conversations, 2, 43–44
Discussing, 11, 23, 31, 35, 43, 46, 53, 55, 61, 66, 69, 70, 72
Explaining, 18, 49, 58
Interrupting to clarify, 6
Interviewing, 5, 11, 73
Rating your speaking, 39, 77
Reporting to class, 67

Role playing, 5, 11, 29, 30, 39, 44, 56, 68, 73, 77
Telling stories, 6, 53, 61

Topics

Making an impact, 40–51
Mysteries, 52–63
Personality, 26–37
Shopping, 19–25
Stories, 2–13
Technology, 14–25
Workplace, 64–75

Viewing

CNN® videos, 11, 23, 35, 49, 61, 73

Vocabulary

Adjectives
Describing generational differences, 40–41
Describing personality characteristics, 26–27, 31
adopt, 53
alibi, 13
ambitious, 37
anecdotes, 12
Antonyms, 36
apathetic, 51
appliance, 25
business, 75
candidate, 50
company, 75
contraption, 25
corporation, 75
describe, 37
determined, 37
device, 25
disinterested, 51
doing well, 75
duties, 51
even though/although/though, 28
excuse, 13
explain, 37
explanation, 13
fables, 12
firm, 75
Forming new words/phrases, 38
gadget, 25
get to the bottom of (something), 15
goof off, 65
gossip, 12
guess, 63
hunch, 63
hunt for, 63
indifferent, 51
internship, 41
irony, 45
lesson, 13

let someone go, 35
look for, 63
make it, 75
message, 13
moral, 13
motivated, 37
Mystery words, 52–53, 62–63
Noun + preposition combinations, 15
Nouns
Compound, 27
Plural, 53
obligation, 51
one of a kind, 25
out of the ordinary, 52
Phrases, 36
Categorizing, 14–15
with *trend*, 24
portray, 37
Prefixes
a-, 41, 51
mal-, 63
over-, 25
un-/il-/im-, 51
public service announcement, 49
pushy, 37
Relationship adverbs, 37
requirement, 51
Responding to speculation, 56
responsibility, 51
run into, 53
salary, 74
to say the least, 53
search, 63
slacker, 40
special, 25
staff, 75
statement, 12
Story words, 2–3, 12–13
succeed, 75
Suffixes, 31
tale, 12
Technology words, 14–15, 24–25
theory, 63
think outside the box, 46
thrive on, 75
uninterested, 51
unique, 25
without equal, 25
Workplace words, 64–65, 74–75

Writing

Charts, 42, 60
Conversations, 42
Definitions, 70
Description, 34
Job application letters, 72

Expansion Pages Answer Key

Unit 1

A. 1. d 2. e 3. c 4. a 5. b **B.** 1. end of story 2. It's the same old story. 3. to make a long story short 4. What's the story?
5. is a different story **C.** 1. anecdotes 2. tales 3. statement 4. yarns 5. a report 6. gossip 7. the fable 8. chronicle **D.** 1. fate
2. expectantly 3. firm 4. solemnly 5. consequences 6. spell

Unit 2

A. a trend toward, the current trend, the upward trend, buck the trend **B.** 1. a trend toward 2. reverse the trend 3. downward trend
4. economic trends 5. setting the trend **C.** 1. f 2. a 3. c 4. g 5. d 6. e 7. b **D.** 1. f 2. c 3. d 4. a 5. e 6. b **E.** 1. overdo it
2. overdue 3. overeat 4. overpowering 5. overlooked 6. overloaded

Unit 3

A. 1. a split personality 2. a personality clash 3. a sports personality 4. a strong personality 5. A personality disorder 6. personality
traits **B.** 1. j 2. e 3. d 4. g 5. a 6. f 7. i 8. h 9. b 10. c **C.** 1. overachiever 2. pushover 3. hothead 4. control freak
D. 1. driven 2. conflict 3. extrovert 4. loud 5. aloof 6. gloomy 7. cautious 8. disappointment **E.** 1. shouldn't 2. seldom 3. a lot
4. wasn't 5. together 6. pay more attention

Unit 4

A. 1. f 2. b 3. a 4. c 5. d 6. e **B.** 1. active 2. an activity 3. proactive 4. an activist 5. acting 6. activism **C.** 1. freezing 2. tiny
3. boiling 4. terrifying 5. enormous 6. horrendous 7. gorgeous **D.** 1. take action 2. swing into action 3. no further action is needed
4. put your ideas into action 5. call for action 6. plan of action **E.** 1. c 2. a 3. b 4. a 5. c

Unit 5

A. 1. e 2. a 3. d 4. f 5. c 6. b **B.** 1. clue, evidence 2. sleuth, investigator 3. puzzle, enigma 4. speculation, hypothesis **C.** 1. d
2. b 3. a 4. e 5. c **D.** 1. malcontent 2. malpractice 3. malfunction 4. malnourished 5. malformed 6. maltreat

Unit 6

A. 1. together 2. behind 3. around 4. into 5. around to 6. along with 7. off **B.** 1. bills 2. intern 3. take off 4. application 5. go
under 6. give up 7. customer 8. give up **C.** 1. d 2. e 3. a 4. b 5. f 6. c **D.** 1. Get to work! 2. We can work it out. 3. Everything
will work out. 4. Don't get all worked up about it. 5. you have your work cut out for you 6. it's in the works **E.** 1. e 2. h 3. g 4. d
5. b 6. a 7. f 8. c